SELF-CARE FOR YOUR APOCALYPSE

THE USER GUIDE YOU NEVER KNEW YOU NEEDED
TO YOUR OWN WELL-BEING

JENNIFER MCCULLOUGH

CONTENTS

FOREWORD

I cannot stress the importance of this book enough.

I have worked as a psychotherapist for over a decade. In that time, I have seen far too many clients fall into a state of collapse and burnout, pushing themselves to the edge for too long without replenishing their inner resources. Why is this so common and accepted?

As human beings, our capacity for self-care is a natural and intuitive process. We all begin to use our inborn coping skills *in utero*: using our hands as pacifiers, curling and stretching, intuitively touching our bodies. As we develop personalities, our capacity for self-care is shaped by the attachments and consciousness of our caregivers, communities, and the societies that surround us. Hopefully, our environment reinforces our natural inborn intuitive coping mechanisms. Unfortunately, the norm seems to be environments where those intuitive mechanisms we need for self-care are not reinforced, and often become unavailable to us.

Too often, we grow up in environments where this intuition becomes unsafe or unavailable, and we have to relearn those self-soothing mechanisms that were our first behaviors as living beings. Perhaps we are surrounded by caregivers who lack their own resourcing and coping mechanisms and are unable to model healthy resilience. We might live in communities that perceive burnout and exhaustion as badges of honor while self-care is viewed as a selfish indulgence.

It is not surprising that the need for connection and a sense of belonging is paramount to our survival –we are primates, social creatures from our earliest dawn. The sudden rise of postmodern, individualist social isolation doesn't magically change that. We were born with the innate capacity to care for ourselves, but we've always depended on others to help meet our physical and emotional needs, not only as individual infants in the modern age, but as a species since the Stone Age.

Too often, masculine-identifying people are conditioned to be stoics, the strong, silent type, the Gary Cooper archetype of manhood that accepts pain and self-denial as the natural price to pay to "be a man," while feminine-identifying people are conditioned to be *human-givers* rather than human-beings, often leaving ourselves last on the list of priorities to attend to – the loving, nurturing mother that kisses wounds and coddles boys and men, the TV mom who stands over her family and watches them eat while she waits until everyone is served before she feeds herself, if she even eats at all. We learn quite quickly what behaviors are accepted and what aspects of our authentic expression will result in social rejection.

Since social rejection can very much feel like social death, we get into the habit of sacrificing our authenticity to maintain our social attachments. We minimize our own needs and prioritize our obligations to others in efforts to keep the connection. Unhealthy attachments can really do a doozy on our capacity to thrive in safe and healthy ways, even if they are not quite "toxic." How often are we expected to say "yes" when we really mean "no," without consideration fot the consequences we face when we keep our truth silent? Holding our truth in takes a toll on the entire system. The circulatory system gets all wonky, the nervous system is constantly overwhelmed, the immune system begins to shut down. Sacrificing our authentic selves is literally a detriment to our survival.

We already know how to take care of ourselves. When we bump our elbow or stub a toe, we instinctively bring our hand to the wound to soothe the *physical* pain, the *physical* wound. We use our voice to make sound – usually a loud one – to assist our natural stress response. The problem lies when our *emotional* pain, our *emotional* wounds, go un-soothed. When our environment expects us to not make a loud sound with our voice to assist our natural stress responses in social situations, we are left with a wound that is not healed.

So what are we to do?

You're holding it.

You are holding, in your hands right now, a precious resource that will help you return to your own intuition and remember your sense of purpose. Intentional self-care is an essential practice that we need in order to keep showing up for ourselves and our people. Jenn has provided us with so many wonderful tools that we can carry with us for the remainder of our journeys.

Welcome back to you.

Kelly Rose, LMFT
Minnetonka, MN
January, 2021

DEDICATION

To my father, because you always knew I had something to
share with the world and you *never* let me forget it.
To my sister Emily, because you told me that I *am* artistic.
To my daughters, Izzy and Sallie, because you showed me
why I had to learn to love myself harder.

A NOTE TO YOU

It's Thanksgiving 2020, and I am writing this at the beginning of our second pandemic "lockdown" here in Minnesota. COVID-19, "19," coronavirus, "The 'Rona"... whatever you call it, it's still going strong.

Masks have been mandated in public spaces here for a while. Restaurants are closed to dine-in customers. Bars and gyms are closed. Public schools have moved to distance-only learning. And... my life isn't much different today than it was a month ago.

My kids have been home since March. My eldest recently became unemployed because she worked as a lifeguard and swim instructor at a public pool. My youngest is home for Thanksgiving because her dad, with whom she was going to spend the day, was exposed to someone who tested positive for the virus earlier this week.

I felt a little bit lame after the first "shelter-in-place" orders expired because I had not started a business, learned a new language, written a book, gotten in peak physical condition, or done anything that seemed significant at first glance. I hadn't been the crafty mom I thought I would be at the beginning of the shutdown. My family hadn't had regular family game nights. I hadn't used all the extra time to finally develop a workout routine I would stick to. All of a sudden, we were allowed back into the world, and what had I done with all the time given to me? I was disappointed in myself.

But then I took another look back. I saw that I had tended to my mental health and helped my kids navigate an unprecedented experience with as little suffering as possible. We had had more family dinners this year than in all past years combined – which means we had had more conversations. I had been home to hug my girls when they cried or got angry about life. They completed the school year online and I continued to support my clients. We were together even if we didn't know what would happen next. I drove them crazy with my talk of energy and self-care, and we had more family time than ever before. I did not do *nothing*.

I work with between twenty and forty clients per week on average and am beyond blessed to have this work. I know how many people are out of work and it is certainly not lost on me how many people are doing more difficult work than I am. Sometimes it takes my breath away. Through my work, I notice how many people are struggling with how to put themselves at the top of their own priority lists.

I know that, to put ourselves at the top of our own lists, we have to take better care of ourselves. You're taking the first step by reading this book! It'll help you to lay a solid foundation that will benefit you now and in the future, when things may be simpler again.

What I have learned about myself this year is that I do better with this slower pace many of us have been forced into and I want to maintain it when the world shifts into a faster gear – which it eventually will. But for some, this pandemic has created a pace that takes some getting used to. If that's you, you most likely need some version of triage self-care now. By "triage self-care," I mean whatever you need to do to get some equilibrium back, to feel more like yourself, the way you want to be.

If you're struggling to find your footing in the pace of life created by the pandemic, I get it. Sometimes it can feel daunting when you want to make future plans. Other times it may feel like the days and weeks last forever, fly by, and blend together, all at the same time. I've heard someone say it's the longest shortest year they've ever lived. For a lot of things we had thought we had under control, we are now realizing... maybe we don't.

We've all, every single one of us, been tested in many ways this past year, and mental health is on my mind. Self-care is what we all need more of to improve our mental health right now. While this book is written during a pandemic, the words in it stand true for regular times, and my hope is that these words will encourage you to take care of yourself for the rest of your life.

WELCOME. SO GLAD YOU'RE HERE

*C*an I tell you something? I still feel awkward when I use the term "self-care." More on that later.

Still here? Oh good. I share that so you know that I'm still working on some things too. If I could find a magical term that I love to say instead of "self-care," I would use it.

Enough about me, though. Let's talk about you.

If I asked you what you like to do for fun, how long would your list be?

I bet you'd have to think on that one.

What if I asked you what your favorite way to indulge yourself is?

Crickets?

How about if I asked you to tell me the last time you spent an hour just doing whatever made you feel good?

I had a coach ask me those questions many years ago and I couldn't even come up with one answer. Okay, that's not totally true. I did try to pass off exercise as self-care. Which it is, definitely. But it was the only thing I did that even remotely resembled self-care and, if I was being totally honest, I didn't always find time for it. Can you relate?

apocalypse
> noun
> apoc·a·lypse | \ ə-ˈpä-kə-ˌlips \
> *plural* apocalypses

When I started writing this book, I looked up the Merriam-Webster definition of "apocalypse" because I felt like I might be using it wrong in the title.

When I was reading the definition, my reaction to the first meaning was, "Oh... nope... this isn't a religious book."

1a: one of the Jewish and Christian writings of 200 b.c. to a.d. 150 marked by pseudonymity, symbolic imagery, and the expectation of an imminent cosmic cataclysm in which God destroys the ruling powers of evil and raises the righteous to life in a messianic kingdom

But I kept reading...

2a: something viewed as a prophetic revelation

... still not quite right... kept reading...

3a: a large, disastrous fire

... definitely not... still hopeful...

b: a great disaster

... ahhh... a great disaster... that was more along the lines of what I was thinking. As I write this during the COVID-19 pandemic, we have been experiencing a great disaster, and this was my initial thought about what the word "apocalypse" meant.

I was still drawn to a portion of the first meaning though...

"... destroys the ruling powers of evil and raises the righteous to life..."

Yeah. That's it. That is what I mean when I use "apocalypse" in the title. I recognize I'm taking some poetic license here and ask for your understanding if you're a scholar of apocalyptic writings or have strong feelings for the first definition!

It is my greatest hope that through your experience of reading this book and growing through the activities, you will unapologetically (without apology) destroy the ruling powers (social conditioning and your mindset) of evil (not serving you) and raise the righteous (your already-amazing self) to life.

SO WHY SELF-CARE FOR YOUR APOCALYPSE?

As I mentioned earlier, I have often struggled with the term "self-care" because it sometimes sounds very unattainable to me. Other times, I feel it has been overused and we have become desensitized to it, assuming it's for other women.

Some people call it "self-love." Others may say "self-compassion." If you're also someone who struggles with the term "self-care," pick an alternate word or phrase that works for you and feel free to use that term any time you see "self-care."

Self-care is whatever you need it to be. It is asking yourself, "What do I need right now?" and being willing to give yourself whatever that is. Sometimes it is calm and sometimes it is not. It can be quiet, and it can be loud.

Self-care is all the things you usually think of – meditation, exercise, healthy diet – but it is also leaving the job that eats your soul. It is exiting a relationship that is damaging to your heart. It is knowing when it is time to shift your friend group. It is teaching your kids to give you some space. It is asking for help when your partner is letting you take on the lion's share of work. It is believing that you do not have to hit bottom to change your life. It is knowing that burnout isn't the only turning point. It is trusting yourself.

Self-care is setting boundaries, saying "no" instead of "yes" when you do not want to do something, using kind language to yourself, nourishing your mind and body, allowing yourself to do nothing, saying "yes" to things you deserve even if you are the only one who will benefit, giving yourself grace and flexibility... and it is also facials, massages, and getting your hair done.

Maybe right now, self-care for you is eating a pizza while binge-watching your favorite Netflix series. Perhaps it is taking care of all your medical appointments. It could be intense exercise for an hour a day, every day.

When I reflect on how much I have done since I decided I was my own priority – *holy shit*. Since making this decision, I have created the life I want, and I still have more to do. Now that I prioritize self-care, I am out of corporate. I am my own boss. I am not in an unhealthy marriage. I sold a house because the memories were overwhelming, and it never really felt like home. I moved into a rental – on a lake – because I want the freedom to just be a tenant for a minute. I took care of myself while I grieved the loss of my brother. I get to coach for one of the most amazing companies I could imagine. I actively choose who is in my life and who is not. I am vigilant at the door of my mind.

Of course, sometimes self-care can seem like nothing is happening. Have you ever shot an arrow from a bow? What happens if you don't draw the bow back first? The arrow falls to the ground at your feet.

While the drawing back of the bow literally pulls the arrow further from the target, it is necessary to the success of the arrow. Similarly, if we don't take the time to nurture and nourish ourselves (pull the arrow back), it's much harder, if not impossible, to find our success – whatever that may be.

Self-care can feel dark sometimes. We all have shadows that need healing. It can also feel incredibly bright and frivolous.

Self-care is whatever you need it to be.

Who's to say?

You. Nobody else.

Self-care is *you* taking care of *yourself* – period. Unapologetically.

WHO IS THIS BOOK FOR?

Well, you. If you have it, you need it.

More specifically, I write to you at the point in your life where you are wise enough to know you want something better but aren't sure how to get there.

That is not to say you have not done great things in your life. You have. Even if you can't see them, I know you've done them.

I also know about something called grit. Loosely defined, "grit" is a strength of mind, a strong determination.

Grit is amazing and necessary. It is how we achieve things when we don't have enough energy or time. It's how we get through a busy day after a sleepless night. It's what we use to focus on that work project when we just want to throw our laptop out the window. We use grit to take the high road when we fantasize about throat-punching someone. Grit gets us through the tough spots.

We get shit done. I lived the first forty-plus years of my life in a state of grit – and it's likely I will be there again. Now, through a solid habit of self-care, I have a lot more say about when that will happen.

Many people are living in a state of grit and it is exhausting. Personally, much of what I accomplished in my adult life was achieved through willpower, because I did not know how to nourish my soul and practice self-care. I was the little engine that could: *I think I can, I think I can, I think I can.* I had a rock-star career. I kept trying marriage. I gave my all as a mom. I was the one in my immediate family who helped the others. I was gritty.

I was also fatigued, lonely, and losing sight of why I did anything.

I want you to know that I see you. I see your insecurities and what you think are flaws. I see your beauty, wisdom, and strength. I see your fear and worry. I see you taking care of everyone and everything else in your life. I see you hoping for the next part of life, when you can relax and enjoy the fruits of your labor. I see how you keep looking for the way through. I see you tired and hurting. I see you laughing and loving. I see you doing things just because they need to be done. I see you wondering if this is all there is. I see how you do more than you are asked and give more than you have. I see that you are ready to change that.

I know how to help. And I know it is simpler than you think it will be. Shall we begin?

WHO THE HELL AM I?

I am the woman who did not even know what self-care was ten years ago.

I mean, if someone had asked me to describe it, I would have said it was something people that had a lot of time might do, like yoga poses in nature.

Five years ago, I became the woman who knew what self-care was but definitely didn't have time for it.

I would beat myself up because I couldn't manage my time well enough to do yoga poses in nature. I couldn't even sit still long enough to do yoga in general. As for meditation? You've gotta be kidding – I couldn't empty my mind for more than twenty seconds. I labeled myself a failure at self-care.

Let me back up for a few minutes.

I came by the non-existent-self-care habit honestly, like many of you. I was raised in a family that struggled with alcoholism and mental illness, the eldest of three, then four when my mom remarried later in life. Five, if you count my dad's second-round son, but we didn't grow up together.

My point in sharing that is to note that I took care of a lot of things that were not "me." That was a solid pattern for a long time. I was rewarded for it with more responsibility and the idea that, eventually, I could take a break because all these people would take care of themselves. I definitely had some boundary work to do.

I started college a few times but, since I was not a priority to myself, other things came up and I never finished. I got a job with a bank. My plan was to work there until I figured out what I wanted to do. So, after some pondering, I left... a mere twenty-four years later.

But during those twenty-four years, I was driven to be the best I could be to prove that I was not "less than" anyone who had a college degree. I was constantly looking ahead to see how to get the next promotion... the next raise... and then doing that work before getting paid for it to show I was capable and worthy. I cannot count how many times I was surprised when people listened to me or trusted my judgment. I won awards for my leadership skills – some national, even! And yet I still spent the entire time afraid I would be fired. (I did not know that that was part of the system, because I was *in* the system.)

I never meant to stay that long. Work at the bank was good – really good – for about the first nineteen years. I adored my team. I stayed the last five years for them. I spent the nineteenth year with the goal of making it to the twentieth year.

At some point during the nineteenth year, a friend of mine asked if I would come with her to a day-long women's retreat-type dealie. My first thoughts were along the lines of, *Are you kidding? Sit around with women I don't know and talk about feelings? Gross, I'll pass.* My first (out loud) response to her was "No thanks."

My friend persisted. So I went. (Remember, I had boundary work to do.)

How was it? Life-changing. I am not even embarrassed to

admit that. I didn't yet know it on the day of the event, but I can look back and see that it was the genesis of my transition to a life I love. During the year that followed, I worked with two of the coaches who had presented that day. Through my growth, I realized I wanted to be a coach. So I did what any normal person would do: I used every hour I could squeeze in between my full-time job and raising two young kids (with a husband who worked nights) to get certified as a coach. *And* I kept it a secret from everyone but my sister (I needed her to do my practicum work with, so I *had* to tell her).

"In secret?" you ask. Yes, in secret.

I didn't have the courage to tell anyone else about my new career dreams. I continued to invest in personal development courses and additional coaching certifications until I came up with a plan.

The Plan: I would keep my corporate gig (main breadwinner, nice salary, bonus, benefits, lots of time off, pretty cushy) and coach on the side until I was old enough to retire.

The Reality: The more I coached and began to create my own business, the less I could stomach the corporate job I already did not like. I won't go into full detail here, but I was as miserable as I ever want to be at the end of that job. Tears, migraines, rage... those were typical for my workdays, and carried over into my personal life. (The tears and rage were in private, of course – I *was* still a professional.)

I ended up giving my notice about twenty years earlier than I initially expected to. I left that career with almost no plan. Leaping and hoping for wings on the way down – that was me.

Was I scared? Hell yes. Did I have days I searched LinkedIn for corporate jobs? Absolutely. Did I wonder how I would make Christmas happen for my kids when I had $35 in my bank account? For sure.

Did I go back? Nope.

Why? Because I *need* to take care of myself.

During that transitional period in my life, I had learned about what self-care really is.

It is being able to value yourself enough to be the first thing you take care of – no matter what. I got better and better at doing that until it became a natural part of my life. It is simply what I do now.

As I started coaching – women, mostly – it didn't take long for me to notice a trend. A theme, if you will.

Women do not prioritize themselves when it comes to care and feeding. (There is the exception every now and then, but let's be honest, you are probably not reading this book because you have nailed your self-care!)

Now – in the middle of a pandemic – I am the fucking queen of self-care. I have coached hundreds and hundreds of women to *require* self-care in their lives. If they do not yet, they will soon.

I am forty-eight. I am a single mom of two girls (aged ten and sixteen at the writing of this book). They are freakin' amazing. As I mentioned, I left a twenty-four-year career in corporate leadership and that was probably my biggest self-care move of all. I am a coach. I have three cats (kind of an accident, but they are family). I live in Minnesota right now, but do not plan to forever– it is too cold here in the winter. I have been married and divorced three times. After we went our separate ways, my first husband died by suicide. He was a beautiful soul, but we were too young. Second husband – *ahhh*… last time we spoke (a few years ago), he still blamed me for everything wrong in his life. Third husband – we are amicable and doing our best to be good parents to our daughter.

I am taking a break from marriage.

I am a life-long learner. I tend to take "just one more class" before I do something – to be sure I have what I need. I am working on stopping sooner. I am curious about how things work. It was a spark of interest in how the brain works that started when I was in my corporate role that began the path that brought me here, writing this book to you.

That might sound strange – "*to* you" instead of "*for* you." But that is what I mean to say. I am writing *to* you so I can share things I have learned along my journey.

I have compiled many years of learning and living to create this book. And numerous are the people who have shared their experiences and learning with me, including former and current coaches, therapists and energy workers, every teacher I ever learned from, friends, lovers, family, co-workers, peers, strangers... the list is unending. I have so much gratitude for all the people who have been part of my growth.

I do not take credit for the information in this book, only for the order of the words. Some of this may be familiar to you. Perhaps this is the time you will hear it or read it and be able to take it in and change your life.

I believe if you have picked this book, it is perfect for you. I see you. I write to you. This is my love letter to you. Please accept it and believe you deserve it.

I believe we are all – every single one of us – connected by energy. I believe in the Law of Attraction. I believe in logic. I believe in taking inspired action. I believe in science. I believe the brain is, by far, the most fascinating organ in the universe. I believe it is okay to be wrong. I believe in learning and growth. I believe you have the power to absolutely change your life. I believe you can have anything you desire. I believe we can all feel joy. I believe women will change the world – but first, they must change their own worlds.

I believe you, my friend, need to up your self-care game so you can do just that.

3

HOW TO USE THIS BOOK

*Y*ou could be thinking, "She's telling me how to use a book? Okay, I'm done." *Hang on!* Stay with me here. You may choose to skip my instructions and read this cover to cover in one sitting. If you do that, you'll find that there is a lot of good stuff, and you will laugh a few times.

But, if you want to really change your life, here are some tips:

1. Set aside time each day for the book. I recommend fifteen to thirty minutes at first. That will enable you to integrate what you're learning.
2. ✐ Throughout the book, you'll see this symbol. It indicates a written activity of some sort. Don't read further until you've done the written activity as assigned. Some of you may be tempted to keep reading with the intention to come back to do the activities another time. I know. But trust me, you will get the very most out of your time and this book by doing the written activities as they come

up. Sometimes, that means you might not be reading for a few days. On those days, you can use the time I mentioned in #1 to work on your current activity.

3. Have a notebook dedicated the work you will do in this book. That way you won't have to try to find something you wrote down on a scrap of paper or inside the book. But please, write in the book if you are so inclined.

4. You don't have to read the book cover to cover, but you can. It can also be used as a build-your-own-adventure type of experience. Do it whichever way you will stick with it.

5. Finish the book. Near the end, there is a chapter about ongoing self-care and what I call self-care minimalism. The very last part of the book is a thirty-day challenge from me to you. You're welcome! In the challenge, I guide you to stick to building a self-care habit for thirty days. If you skip some, start over. When you finish thirty days in a row, keep on self-caring and add more. That is how you keep your momentum going.

SENSUALITY AND SELF-CARE

Some of you may not be comfortable with the word "sensuality."

I love it. If you learn to love it, your life will be even better.

Think of it literally: it is using your senses. Sight, hearing, smell, taste, and touch are all important. Think about how nostalgic you get when you smell a certain scent or hear a song from years ago.

You will notice as you go through the self-care that your

senses are mentioned in several spots. The more you connect with as many senses as you can, the better your life will be.

Self-care must be sensual. To fully engage your senses is powerful – learn to do it.

4

MIND-BODY CONNECTION

*S*tick with me during this chapter. It's a bit bookish, but it's important stuff. (Am I the only one cracking up that I called a chapter in a book "bookish"? Probably.)

Moving right along... How cool is it that our thoughts can impact our health? I *love* knowing that.

There's a ton of research available about why taking care of yourself is important. I'm probably not telling you anything new on that front. I'll sum up the benefits and if you want to geek out on more data and information, Google is your spot – have at it!

Super high-level summary: treating yourself to a regular habit of self-care can increase your energy and productivity, and can reduce anxiety and stress.

We all know that stress will suck the life out of you. It steals your sleep. It interrupts your enthusiasm. It eliminates your energy. If left unchecked, it *owns* your health. And stress is a slumlord.

Stress... worry... anxiety... overwhelm... burnout... over-thinking... Whatever word you use for it, it does not serve you at all. But you are probably used to it. It feels natural! That's how it gets you.

Did you know that the brain can't tell the difference between reality and imagination? All the things you stress about, the brain believes those things are really happening as you think about them.

Do this for me: recall a time when you had a dream about someone. This person could be a partner, lover, friend, anyone. In the dream, they were an ass to you, and you were angry. Eventually, you woke up, remembered your dream, knew it was just a dream... but you were still angry at the person. You even had the physical feelings that go along with anger.

What the hell? This is how your brain works, your visual cortex, to be exact. It's like the movie screen of your mind. Powerful stuff.

Not to get too science-y, but thoughts kick off chemicals in the brain. Your feel-good chemicals are dopamine, oxytocin, serotonin, and endorphins. Your stress chemicals are dopamine (yes, it's two-faced), epinephrine or adrenaline, norepinephrine, and cortisol.

Each chemical has a different effect on your nervous system and your body. That warm, tingly feeling you get when you hug someone you love starts with oxytocin. That feeling you get when you are scared – the cold and hot at the same time shock to your system – starts with adrenaline. My only point here is to make the connection that your mind can create a physical reaction.

Over time, the physical reactions created by your mind have an impact on your health. It can be a positive or a negative impact, depending on how you choose to live your life. I know it may not feel like a choice right now, but by the end of this book, after the experiences you will create using the exercises you'll learn, you will know it *is* a choice.

You don't have to be a chemist here – you just have to understand two things:

1. Stress will definitely, no doubt, impact your health in a negative way.
2. You can do something about it.

PRODUCTIVITY MYTH

Most people who come to me for coaching are under the impression (at least at first) that if they aren't being productive, they aren't valuable. I had the same belief system a few years back.

Allow me to shine a light on why we think this way.

See, our economy is designed in a way that requires all of us to produce something – services, products, ideas, etc. If we aren't producing, the economy doesn't grow. From a young age, we are rewarded (or at least, we feel like we're rewarded) for producing. Good grades equal good attention. Bad grades equal less positive attention. A college degree may equal a higher income. Working more hours can equal a promotion – or at least the promise of one in the future. And we're off to the rat race.

I get that I've oversimplified our economy. I'm not an economist, and this isn't that book.

The darker side of this system is that we aren't rewarded for keeping ourselves healthy or taking care of our mental health. The connection that is missing here is if we are not healthy (mind/ body/ soul), we are not producing our best work. But because of the promise of future reward, we are constantly attempting to do so. This is where exhaustion and burnout come up. The promise isn't always real.

We live in the model of "if we do enough, have enough,

give enough, be enough... *then* we will take care of ourselves."

Think of it as a hamster wheel, and you're on it. Running and sweating and barely able to catch your breath... but still increasing your effort.

That is the myth part: working harder to produce more does not make you more valuable. But it keeps you working for "the man." And that is how the wheel works. It's not working for you.

Truth: valuing yourself enough to take care of yourself enables you to be more effective at whatever you do in life. Work, relationships, fun... all of it. You do not always have to be producing.

Doing nothing *is* doing something. Filling your tank so you can keep going is critical.

Believe me when I tell you this: you do not need to be productive all the time. Go back to the hamster wheel imagery. Grab the outside of the wheel and fling yourself off into freedom. Your wings will come.

Now, let's talk about why you think you can't do this. I'll start with time.

INVISIBLE WORKLOAD

It's time to notice the things you do that you do not account for in your schedule. I know about these things because I do them. I also know *you* do them. I can't tell you how many times I have heard a client tell me she did not get much done, disappointment clear in her voice, because she doesn't give herself credit for her invisible workload.

It is the planning... the scheduling... the phone calls... the bills paid... the mental notes... the meals made (and planned and prepped)... the carpools driven... the shopping done... the school supplies purchased (especially the day before the project is due)... the crises averted... the animals cared for... the gifts sent... the cards mailed... all the things you do on the way to switch the laundry...

This is the invisible workload. We don't always include these in our actual schedule, and often it is the woman who carries this load.

I'll share an example from my former life. Let's talk about a road trip. I would pack for myself, arrange for pet care, pack clothes and car activities for both children (until they were old enough to do it themselves), make the hotel arrangements if we were stopping, prepare snacks and drinks for the trip, and make sure it was all ready to go when we wanted to leave. None of that was on my calendar. I fit it all in around a full-time job and parenting while my then-husband worked nights.

The paradigm we lived in was that we were equals. The truth was I was carrying a much heavier load than my husband was. I believed I had to take on that whole invisible workload to prove my value.

I am not saying your situation is exactly the same or that you do all those exact things or that nobody helps. I am saying we typically do not pay attention to the time and energy our invisible workload sucks out of us.

Most things in the invisible workload have to get done. Many of us don't give ourselves credit for doing them or even formally plan for them. It may seem unnecessary, but it's okay to schedule them. By including obligations in your list of what has to get done, you'll begin to notice *everything* you do and won't be left feeling like you're not accomplishing anything.

Later in this book, I go over the idea of a Grit List. When you get to that section, I highly recommend that you start your own Grit List. You won't regret it.

5

WHY NOT?

*H*ere's the part where I crash through all the reasons why you don't put yourself at the top of your priority list.

I'll bet you can't come up with an excuse I haven't heard. (When I say "excuse," understand that I know these are valid reasons why you don't prioritize your own care in your life right now!)

I'll start off by sharing some of the many excuses I used to make to not take care of myself (remember what I shared about where I was ten years ago?). See how many are familiar to you.

Keep in mind, some of these were conscious and some subconscious reasons. We are conditioned as women to take care of others first. It's practically in our DNA.

Here's my list:

1. I never had a role model for taking care of myself
2. No time
3. Too tired after taking care of everything else
4. Not enough energy

5. Did not care
6. "I will start tomorrow/ next week/ next month/ next year"
7. Did not know it was important
8. Knew it was important, but "I am young – there is time for it later"
9. Did not have the patience to slow down
10. Afraid of what others would think if I took a break – ever
11. Felt like I was failing if I was not being productive
12. Concerned I would get behind and not be able to catch up with my endless responsibilities
13. Got some kind of positive reinforcement when I took care of others
14. Got some kind of negative reinforcement when I did not
15. The utter and complete feeling of stress I'd feel the whole time if I took time for myself
16. "People in my life need me to be available every second"
17. "If I am not available, something catastrophic will happen and I will have to deal with that!"
18. Did not love myself enough
19. Did not understand how to take care of myself
20. Got even more stressed when I took time for myself
21. "Self-care is selfish"
22. "I am not important enough to take the time"
23. "There is so much to do!"

… And on and on and on and on.

––––––

✎ You may have other reasons. Go ahead and write them down in your notebook. Give some thought to this one. You do not have to solve it, just be aware of it.

––––––

Truth: The only reason self-care is not happening in your life is because you are not making it important enough.

Neither was I.

Before you can make self-care a priority, you are going to have to learn how to say "no" to some of the things you say "yes" to now. Ya with me?

6

THE POWER OF "NO"

*S*aying "no" is the most important self-care in the whole universe. In fact, if you cannot say "no," it'll be hard to add time for yourself to your calendar.

We are conditioned from a young age to say "yes" to everyone else, even when we do not want to say it. Sometimes *especially* when we do not want to say it.

We have learned to say "yes" to everyone else's priorities, and that takes up all our self-care time.

The wonderful thing is that you can change that.

EVOLVE YOUR "NO"

Learning to say "no" is no different than building a muscle. Remember, our "yes" muscles are pretty strong, so the first few times we say "no" when we would have typically said "yes"... *ugh!* They can be so hard. When I started exercising my "no" muscle, I would get nauseous and shaky, and those feelings would last for a while after I said it, like there were going to be serious repercussions.

At first, "no" might sound like:

- "Um... well... I do not think so... but maybe."
- "No????"
- "I am really sorry... I would... I am so busy... oh... well... I guess if I switch some things around..."
- "I can't... I am sorry... wait... let me check on something..."
- "No... I feel terrible... I wish I could help..."
- "Oh... sure, I guess."
- "Yeah... I can do that."
- "Fine."

———

✎ Take a minute to think about the words you use instead of "no." Go ahead and write those down in your notebook.

———

Through my own growth and research of many, many women, I realized it is the emotion we tie to our "no" that causes all the drama.

Hear this: nothing has any meaning but the meaning we give it. Write that down. It is crazy helpful as you build your "no" muscle. *Nothing has any meaning but the meaning we give it.*

And we have given a hell of a lot of meaning to what will happen if we say "no." Let's take a look at that meaning.

WHY WE SAY "YES" WHEN WE MEAN "NO"

We give meaning to what will happen if we say "no." When you start to unpack this, you will notice that, for the most part, *you* are the reason you say "yes" when you want to say "no." Through your life experiences, you have created a belief system around what will happen if you say "no." The keyword there is "belief." It's not fact.

There are so many reasons we *think* we need to say "yes." I will list the most common ones I have come across in my work here.

- "I can help them."
- "I should help them."
- "Who will do it if I do not?"
- "I can't say 'no.'"
- "I am supposed to say 'yes.'"
- "They need me."
- "I am the only one who can do this."
- "I was raised this way."
- "They will be angry if I do not do it."
- "I will hurt their feelings."
- "I want to be a good friend/ partner/ person."
- "I have no idea."

———

✎ Stop here and go make a list of all the people you say "yes" to when you want to say "no," and write your reason next to each name. Use one page per person because you will be writing more about those relationships in the next sections. Do not keep reading and think you will come back to this – it doesn't work that way. Go write!

———

WHAT IS THE COST OF YOUR "YES"?

Over time, there is a cost for saying "yes" when you want to say "no." I will share a silly story to illustrate this. It'll sound as if it is of no importance in the grand scheme of things, but it was profound in my recognition that I had to learn to say "no."

This happened about six or seven years ago. I was on the couch reading – studying something, I don't even remember what now. My daughter – who was around eight or nine at the time – called out from her bedroom and asked me if I would make a sandwich for her.

My reaction was immediate and so, so, *so* dramatic. I was totally pissed. I rolled my eyes. Slammed my book shut. Tossed it on the floor. Got up and huffed into the kitchen. I grabbed the bread and threw it on the counter, stomped to the refrigerator and pulled out the ham, cheese, condiments… I angrily made a sandwich *at* my daughter, the whole time grumbling about how she could totally make her own sandwich. *What was she thinking? Did not I do a better job raising her?*

Yeah, I had some issues, many of which were symptoms of a life saying "yes" when I needed to say "no."

So I made my daughter a sandwich. I yelled at her to come get it. She was perplexed about why I was being such a jerk. She was confused, and most likely hurt at my reaction. *WHAT?* I wondered to myself. *I had said "yes!"*

Fortunately, I had a coach at the time, and I was working on being present with my kids so I could enjoy life more. Because of that, I was able to give some thought to my reaction. My daughter was not an ass for asking for a sandwich. I was an ass for not saying "no."

I know this because the next time my daughter asked, I just answered that I was in the middle of something, and she made her own sandwich without even blinking. Bonus: by doing that, I had just taught my daughter that my time was important too – and because I am her role model, she also believes that *her* time is important.

Does that mean everyone is always okay when you say "no"? Nope. That is not the moral of the story.

———

Before we move into the next section, go back to that list of people you say "yes" to when you mean "no" and write down the effect that is having on that relationship. Think about the impact on you, on the other person, and on the relationship as a whole. Really ponder this. Be honest with yourself. Nobody is going to see your list but you. Maybe you have had feelings about this before, but you had never connected them to the fact that you value other peoples' priorities over your own. It's something to think about!

I will leave a few potential relationship effects for you:

- Relationship damage
- Lowered confidence
- Fatigue
- Confusion in relationships
- Mental health issues
- Really bad time management
- Lack of fulfillment
- Confusion about your identity
- Superficial relationships
- Resentment
- Health issues
- Lowered energy

I'll give you an example. Remember that sandwich I rage-made in my earlier story? It would look like this in my notes:

Who: My daughter

Reasons I Don't Say "No": I can and should help her. It will hurt her feelings if I say "no." It's not that difficult to make a sandwich. *(Notice: the first two are inaccurate in the sandwich situation… but I believed them.)*

Impacts: Resentment, putting my priorities last, interrupting my time, hurting my daughter's feelings

Okay, so now you should have a nice list going – including people, reasons, and impacts. If you do not, trust me, you want to have that list. Go back and write it before reading on.

————

To live your best life – which may be a life you are just starting to imagine or one you have dreamed about for years – you must protect yourself. You must value your time and energy *more* than those of other people.

Your priorities must come first. For that to happen, you are going to have to say "no" to other people to protect your priorities.

Step one, think of it like this: you are not saying "no" *to* someone else, you are saying "no" *for* yourself. For protection of your future.

Remember a few sections back when you worked on what meaning you were giving if you said "no"? Here is where we start to take that meaning out of saying "no." By doing that, we can remove some, if not all, of the emotion you tie to it.

There are two aspects to "no": who and how. *Who* are you saying "no" to and *how* powerful you need your "no" to be?

Let's talk about the "who" first. Imagine your protection as a bubble, a forcefield, a wall… whatever works for you. Understanding *who* you are dealing with helps you to know how much you need to protect your "no."

THE "WHO" OF YOUR "NO"

Most of the people in your life will fall into the following categories:

- Family
- Friends
- Co-workers/ boss
- Acquaintances
- Energy zombies posing as any of the other categories

Most of these groups are self-explanatory, so I'm going to focus mainly on the energy zombies. Know this: a zombie just needs to eat a brain. They do not care whose brain. This is *super* important to believe.

You with me? Okay. So we all have people in our lives – family, friends, even people we work with – who are energy zombies. You will know who they are because you feel drained around them. The relationships are lopsided, you give more than they do, they are not respectful of your life, and they consistently ask you to do things for them... be things for them... give things to them. Can you think of any energy zombies in your life? I know you can. They're everywhere.

The thing is, if they must stop eating your brain because you won't let them, they'll find another one. They will move on to the next willing soul. That might seem gross and dramatic, but it's true. Ask anyone who has successfully implemented "no."

For everyone *except* energy zombies, you can use a pretty low level of protection. Energy zombies, though, get the brick wall.

Did any of you relax just a touch there? This concept is

pretty simple. I did not say "easy," but it is *simple*. That is the "who" aspect of "no."

🖋 Go back to your list of people and label them. They all fit into one of these categories – maybe two if they're energy zombies – guaranteed.

THE "HOW" OF YOUR "NO"

Here is the "how" aspect, meaning how powerfully you stand behind your "no."

Sticking with the protection idea, the more detail you include in your "no," the less powerful it will be and the less you are protecting your own time and energy.

When I say "detail," I mean explanation… reasons… excuses… justifications… all the ways we try to make ourselves feel better when we say "no." Detail weakens your protection.

I will give you an example. Imagine that I have both a dear friend and an energy zombie asking for my time and energy on a day when I am unable to accommodate their requests.

To my dear friend, I would say, "You know what? I can't meet you in person, but how about we jump on the phone? If that does not work, this is when I can meet."

To the energy zombie, I would respond, "No. I have other plans." (Pro-tip: "other plans" can literally just be not doing what they're asking of me.)

And before I stop thinking about the request, the energy zombie will have moved on to the next person on their list –

because they have a mental *list* of brains they're allowed to eat.

Make sense? I can trust a dear friend to respect my time and energy so I can feel comfortable giving details. Sometimes I even want to leave some wiggle room.

I do not even entertain the idea of giving an energy zombie a way through my protection, so no detail is required. I will just say "no" – if I respond at all.

Also, "no" is a complete sentence. And when you get comfortable with it, you will say it to dear friends and family without any twitching – on your part or theirs.

Again, those are the two aspects of "no": who and how.

Who are you saying "no" to? How much detail will you provide? It is not emotional. It is logical.

Circling back to the evolution of "no." Something really amazing happens once you get comfortable saying "no" to people: your "no" power evolves. Remember how I said it's like a muscle? The more you work it, the stronger it gets. You will begin to say "no" to other things, situations that are not in alignment with your vision. The more you say "no" to other peoples' priorities, the more you begin to value yourself. The more you value yourself, the more life expands in front of you.

———

✍ Categorize your list of people as they relate to the protection idea. Detail or no detail? If "yes" to detail... how much?

———

You are building the foundation for your "no" power... go do it!

WHAT NOW?

Alrighty… what now? Let's put it into action! If you just want to go start saying your "no"s, more power to you. But for more ease while you create a new habit, how about some tips? Success leaves clues, right? Let me tell you what has worked for me and many of my clients.

There are four steps to building your "no" muscle.

First step: purpose. *Why* are you building your "no" muscle? This is your emotional juice, your superpower for when it gets hard.

Second step: prepare. Just like any time we try to change anything, without preparation, no go.

The third step is practice. Yup. You have to *practice* saying "no." Out loud.

The penultimate step: pay attention. So many of us are on autopilot.

Once you have found your purpose, prepared, practiced, and paid attention… you are ready to *protect*, the final step! That is the best part. That is when the magic starts to happen.

You can protect:

- Your physical health
- Your schedule
- Your priorities
- Your mental health
- Your dreams
- Your relationships
- Your energy
- Your future
- Your thoughts
- Your emotions
- Your energy

- Your time

Notice a theme there?

PURPOSE

Purpose: why are you learning to say no?

This is where you want to give meaning. The emotional connection will be your fuel. When you have a big enough purpose, you can do anything.

You are the one to stand guard at the door of your mind. You choose your own priorities and give your own meaning.

You get to choose when to say "yes" and when to say "no." Choose wisely. This purpose will help you to do that.

———

Take some time for yourself and write down your reasons why you need to protect yourself. Get detailed. Make it a special exercise. Light a candle... play some music... grab your favorite beverage... and imagine what your life will be when you are true to yourself and use your "no." Write yourself a story about how your life will be when you put yourself first on your list of priorities.

Here's an example:

I start the day fully rested and looking forward to what's on my schedule. I take some time to meditate and really appreciate that the kids know how important it is for me to have this time in the morning. I enjoy my breakfast with them and then head to my office. I pop off an email to reschedule an appointment so I can have some extra time for planning the family vacation coming up. I make plans with a friend to meet after work each day and work out together. I get an urgent text from a friend who seems to always be in a state of emergency. She's asking for help tonight. I respond that I can't – I have plans already. She's fine. I double-check my calendar for the week. I've cleared my weekend because I want to go with the flow and I'm really looking forward to it. After my last client appointment, I run my kids to the dentist then home for dinner. They work on homework while I relax. I help them problem-solve if they need it but they also know how to email their teachers for help beyond what I can do. Before bed, I watch a program with my youngest, tuck her in, and then it's into my room for my nightly routine. My head is on the pillow in time for plenty of rest.

———

PREPARE

The next thing you are going to do is get your supplies ready. You are going to sit down and brainstorm all the different ways you can say "no."

Think about how many times you have decided to eat healthy. As long as you prepare your food ahead of time... *golden!* But those days when you don't... you still eat, right? Just not necessarily the food you need.

How about exercise? Are you more likely to show up for a class you signed up for or a fitness appointment you made, or are you more likely to go work out at the gym when nobody knows you will be there?

Planning and preparing make a huge – if not the total – difference in your success. You can prepare your "no"s. What will you say? You have that great list now, the who and the how.

There is a technique to this part of the process, too.

You must be in the right frame of mind to prepare. If "no" does not come naturally, you need to create the space for yourself for even just that preparation. Set aside some time, say thirty minutes to an hour. Make sure you're not tired during this preparation time. Grab your favorite beverage, light a candle if that's your thing, play some good music, and get ready to enjoy your preparation. You are preparing to have the life you want. Close your eyes and imagine your life if you only said "yes" when you meant it. Would your shoulders drop? Would you have less tension in your neck? Would you smile more? The goal here is to get yourself ready to say "no."

Grab some index cards. There is something about writing by hand that drills things into the nervous system differently. *Anyhoo*, sitting in your nice space... music playing... candle lit... write your heart out.

Here's the beauty of brainstorming: there is no such thing as a wrong idea. Think of all the times you wish you had said "no" in the past. Say it on the index cards now. It does not need to be specific to any person or situation. You are not matching your "no"s to people yet! Do not judge. Do not question. Do not doubt. Do not criticize. Just write. There will be time for weeding out later. In fact, make it a game. See how many ways you can come up with to say "no"!

Here's the biggest rule: do not justify your "no."

Justifying is when you give details because you are uncomfortable saying "no." It is fine to give details if you want to negotiate, but giving details because you're uncomfortable is a slippery slope.

When you are writing and you start to explain yourself... stop and think. Learn *your* difference between justifying and providing appropriate detail. Keep in mind that giving detail is like giving out keys to your protection; the more you give, the easier it is for the person to get to your "yes."

I will leave some ideas here:

- "No, but thanks for thinking of me."

- "I can't do that. But I can help with X!"
- "I have other plans."
- "Nope. I am in the middle of something."
- "No thanks."
- "Hell no."
- "No."
- "I can't. I hope you find someone who can."
- (No response at all.)

When I was first starting out, I used I have other plans *a lot*. Even if my other plans were just to not do what I was being asked to do! Remember, "no "is a complete sentence and no response is absolutely acceptable in some situations.

———

✎ Go! Come back when you have a stack of cards. Do not worry if that takes a few days. This book will still be here.

———

PRACTICE MAKES PERFECT

So you have your list of "no"s. You also have your list of people you need to say "no" to sometimes. Soon, you will get to marry the two lists. But first, *how* you practice is important.

Do not trick yourself into believing you can just go forth and say "no" without practice. Trust me. I know you may not practice at first – I didn't – but then you will remember this moment and you *will* practice. Remember, this is not emotional. We do not need to be emotional about our "no"s. That is where the practice helps.

At first, your "no"s may sound hesitant, perhaps defensive

or unsure. That's normal! The first time you walked (I know you don't remember!), you fell down. I don't even need to know you to say that. In the same way, the first time you say "no" you will trip over it. That is why it matters that you practice. In front of your bathroom mirror. In the shower. In your car. I am not picky about where... just do it.

This is science. It works for you and against you. Our brains have kept us safe – well, alive, anyway – up 'til now. The brain likes status quo. That is why it is hard to change, well, anything. Our brains are like, *Um... nope.* (See, you are good at saying "no," you just don't realize it yet!)

Your job now is to teach the brain a different way. You need to practice out loud. A lot.

Step One: Read your cards from the Prepare step out loud a couple times a day. Notice how you feel when you read them. Some will feel better than others. Notice, also, how you get smoother at saying your "no"s.

Step Two: After a couple days, pick the cards that feel the most like you. But do not throw the other ones away!

Step Three: Read the cards you picked out loud a couple times a day for a few days. Again, notice your feelings.

Step Four: Stop reading and start *saying*. Speak from the heart. Say your "no"s in front of the mirror. Say them in the shower. Say them in the car. Just say them!

Go ahead and match your "no"s to your list of people and situations, keeping in mind that your details and explanations are not for the energy zombies. This takes practice to another level. You can always come back to this if you try to start saying "no" without matching your "no"s to actual people and it does not work for you. Once you have matched "no"s to people, then continue practice them out loud, but imagine the person you've matched to each "no" being there. This step is a must for your more difficult relationships.

I am even going to leave some more ideas here for you.

- "That does not fit into my schedule."
- "That sounds overwhelming. I hope you get it figured out."
- "I am working on a lot myself. Who else can help?"
- "I am not ready to do that. Thank you for understanding."
- "Not today. Perhaps another time."
- "It does not feel like a hell yes – so, no."

––––––

✍ Spend about five to ten minutes a day practicing your "no"s out loud. You can move on to the next step if you want, but keep practicing.

––––––

PAY ATTENTION

Remember how at the beginning of the chapter I told you that the main reason I said "yes" was just habit? Well, habits do not change without our awareness. You have to pay attention. To your body... to your breath... to your thoughts and emotions. I will give you some tricks a little later. The body is key – it never lies.

How do you feel when you say "yes" when you want to say "no"? Not just during the conversation, but how do you feel about the person you continually say "yes" to?

Notice what happens to your body. Even when our brains try to tell us everything is okay, our bodies will tell the truth. As you go through your days, pay attention. When you approach a conversation with someone and you know you usually give a "yes" when you mean "no," your body will warn you ahead of time. What is that like? Notice.

Your body will even holler at you when you get a text or email from someone. Do you feel good, or did your stomach drop? I will give you some advice: if your body is feeling sick about responding to someone, it is time to pause. Pay attention. You might not change your answer just yet, but grow that awareness. Awareness is a gift during times of change. I will also share that not responding is absolutely within your rights. You are not required to respond to someone simply because they've contacted you. Know that.

Pay attention before, during, and after the interaction, whether it is in person, in writing, or on the phone. What happens afterward? Are you relieved? Excited? Happy? Relaxed? How do you feel?

You are feeling good if you answered in a way that's true to yourself. If you feel dread, stress, tension, unease... that means your "yes" should be a "no." Remember my story about the sandwich for my daughter – I had all those feelings. I should have said "no." If it is about more than just a sandwich, the feelings and thoughts are much bigger.

The length of time you have been denying yourself a "no" also plays into your reactions. We teach people how to treat us, and if we have taught them poorly for a long time, we are bound to have stronger reactions.

So pay attention. It is important to take note, even journal, during this phase. It may take a few weeks – months even, depending on the frequency of your interactions – to really have a handle on how you react in any given situation. Once you know, that is when you will recognize the importance of the next phase of your "no" work: the actual protection.

———

✍ Go to your list and make some notes about how you feel right now. Then continue to pay attention!

———

PROTECT

It is time to protect yourself. It is time to say "no" out loud (or type it... however the opportunity arises). You will find that a majority of people do not really react when you say "no," because they know it is your right. Pay attention. Let that be wind in your "no" sails. Also pay attention if someone reacts strongly. It is a good indication there is something unhealthy going on!

Keep in mind that when you are working to build muscles, you cannot go to the gym once or three times. You cannot only go on walks for a week then stop. You cannot swim two laps and call it done.

You must keep going. When you keep going, your "no" will evolve into something amazing.

You may start with a "well, maybe" as your "no." But if you keep following the prepare, practice, pay attention, and protect process, eventually you will have a "hell no" pop into your brain.

Sooner than you think, the shakes and sweats go away. They are replaced with a deeper knowledge that your "no" is for the greater good. That might sound dramatic today. I get it.

But pay attention. You will have more time. More energy. More purpose.

After a while, your "no"s grow and become "no, this boss isn't for me... " or "no... this relationship isn't for me" when before, you would have settled for whatever it is that isn't working for you.

Your "no"s evolve until you cannot do something if it does not take you a step closer to your dreams.

When your "no" doesn't feel strong, what will help push you through it? Write that thing down on a sticky note and stick it somewhere you will see it while you are building your muscles.

Now... go forth and use your words! Well, one word specifically: *NO!*

7

READY FOR SOME SELF-CARE?

READY?

*L*et's get clear on *why* self-care will be a priority for you. Pick one reason or ten... but pick something.

Start to condition these new reasons by speaking them out loud.

Do it. Trust me.

Here are some examples:

1. I teach people how to treat me.
2. If I do not value my time and my health, nobody else will do it for me.
3. I attract things and people to me that match my energy. I want a higher-vibe life.
4. I want my son/ daughter/ friend/ mother/ spouse/ lover/ family to see that it is okay to take care of themselves.
5. I want to do more in life, and I need more energy, enthusiasm, and excitement to get that done.

6. I want to live a pain-free life with as much health as I can have.
7. I want to sleep better.
8. I want to laugh more.
9. I deserve to get the very most out of life.
10. I want more free time.
11. I can strengthen my immune system.
12. I deserve to be more confident.
13. I want to grow and learn.
14. I am ready to heal my trauma.
15. I will be able to give, do, and be even more than I am now.
16. I want incredibly connected relationships.

And on and on and on and on.

For a moment, pick your top reason(s) to prioritize self-care and close your eyes. Imagine how that will feel. Connect with the emotions of living life that way. Breathe them in. You can have that.

I will share a story, probably the genesis of my self-care journey. I was working with my first coach and she asked me to pick an emotion, one I did not feel often but wanted to be able to tap into regularly. The best feeling I could think of at the time was peace of mind. That was the absolute top of the pile for me, something I rarely experienced.

At first, it was difficult for me to feel peace of mind. I had to imagine what it might be like. I could get a little spark of it, and that was enough to begin the work.

Peace of mind is still important to me, but it is my standard – my default emotion – now. If I do not have peace of mind, I am going to do something about it. Through years of self-care and growth, I have learned how to tap into any emotion I desire – including joy and ecstasy. I would have been too embarrassed to say those words five years ago!

Now my life is full of joy. I have even been able to keep it up during this pandemic. Of course, some days I have still had to ask myself if I have slipped across the sanity line! *(Then I answer myself that someone who is insane probably would not think to ask.)*

I am not saying we cannot have lower-vibe days. No way! We have them and we honor them. But we have a choice in how we care for ourselves. In fact, I use low-vibe days to up my self-care dosage.

So back to you and your connection to your reason to put self-care at the top of your priority list. If your connection is weak right now, that's okay. I am going to help you build that muscle so you can flex it at will.

Start by coming up with your purpose for self-care.

✎ Tap into your imagination and feel the emotions you will have when you are well-rested, excited about life, and have all the time you need to get things done. Relax your shoulders... your jaw... your neck. Breathe deeply and just imagine. Play it like a movie on your visual cortex. See it in color, hear the sounds, feel the relaxation... enjoy it.

Now go do that. Go on. Do not keep reading until you have done it.

Okay, you're back. Answer these questions. Answer them as if you are living your best self-care life... in present tense.

- What does it feel like?
- What does it mean to you?

- Who have you become in the process?
- Who else does it benefit?
- How?
- What can you do now that you could not do before?

Nice! The coolest part of this exercise is that when you do it again later – after you have been self-caring for a while – it is even *more* awesome.

I will share mine, so you have an example:

- *What does it feel like?* I feel amazing. I feel strong and relaxed at the same time. I feel clear and focused. I feel so much love.
- *What does it mean to you?* I only do things if they are in line with who I am and what I want in life. I have strong boundaries that create structure in my life. The structure allows more fluidity than I have ever had before.
- *Who have you become in the process?* I am so much more of me! I am proud and humble at the same time and I am full of joy! I am the creator of my own life. I serve more people than I ever imagined I could.
- *Who else does it benefit?* Everyone in my life, but mostly my daughters. They see that I am my own priority and they still get everything they need from me. They know mental health is important. They take mental health days. They are better for it!
- *What can you do now that you could not do before?* EVERYTHING I WANT! I ask myself, "What would make me feel better?" and just do whatever

that is. It is so natural now that it just flows in my
life – work and personal – balanced and beautiful!

That right there is a purpose. That is my why.

––––––

🖊 Now, take some time to write your own why. Get
emotionally connected to it. Feel the feelings. Use your
senses.

––––––

While the "why" is critical, I *finally* figured out that no matter
how badly someone wants or needs self-care, without the
"how" it takes way longer than necessary to create a habit.

That is what the rest of the book is about.

SET?

After this chapter, the rest of the book is *full* of ideas for self-
care. Use them.

I want to make sure you have no excuses, so I have
provided enough self-care suggestions that I know for sure
that some – and maybe all – will work for you. The list is not
all-inclusive. You can add more. But definitely use this book
to get going and gain momentum. Do not wing it.

Like I shared, I have coached hundreds of women through
this process, so stick with me – it will work. It is not magic.
You must make the effort. When you have a powerful
purpose, you will make the effort, and it is magical once it is
going.

We are going to have to condition your brain for this. The

super cool part about that is I know how to do it! It is like lifting weights. You don't start by deadlifting three-hundred pounds, you start smaller and build up.

That is exactly what we are going to do. Give me five minutes a day and I will change your life.

———

Grab your calendar. And your phone. (Or just your phone if that is where your calendar is.)

Do it now. This is a "now" thing.

Step 1: Find a five-minute slot of time each day for the next week. It can be a different time each day if that is easier.

Step 2: Block it off for "Me Time" (or whatever you want to call it).

Step 3: Each morning, when you are looking at your phone (because we all do that), double-check that your "Me Time" is still blocked, pick a self-care activity from the "Five Minutes" chapter, and set an alarm* on your phone for that time.

Step 4: When your alarm goes off, no matter what, enjoy your five minutes to their fullest.

Step 5: Repeat until you realize you are looking forward to the five minutes so much that you add another five minutes into your day. You can have as many five-minute "Me Time"s as you want! One an hour! Two an hour! Keep going.

*Pro-tip: title the alarm something amazing like "5 minutes that will make me feel awesome and change my life!"

You may be twitchy at first. You may not feel the effects right away. You may get annoyed with yourself because you are not "doing it right." There is no right way to do it, so stop getting annoyed with yourself. That is the opposite of self-care. You may forget to do it one day – or three. Start again. Keep starting again.

When you have nailed the five minutes and you are feeling good about taking that time, up it to fifteen minutes. Repeat steps one through five, but for fifteen minutes this time.

When you have got fifteen minutes of Me Time going strong, move on to thirty minutes. You can sprinkle fives and fifteens in, too. Start playing with the time. The idea is to have enough structure that you can be fluid. It is not a to-do list and it is not carved in stone. The only requirement is that you take time every day for you.

———

✎ Go ahead and look at your schedule for the next week or so. Schedule a few five-minute spots… maybe even a fifteen-minute spot. Bold! Once you've done that, you have the tiniest glimmer of the beginnings of a new habit. You're awesome!

———

GO!

Keep this book handy. Take notes. Highlight stuff. Fold the page down or bookmark when you find something you love. Use sticky notes for labels if that will help you. Let this book guide you.

As mentioned, you will begin your journey in the "Five Minutes" section.

You can either start at the beginning of the section and try all of the activities in order, or randomly pick a page and do that. You can start at the end of the section and go backward.

You can try a few and pick a favorite and just do that every day. You can do whatever you want, as long as you spend the time on yourself. This is true for all sections.

I have one client who adores the five-minute hand massage with lotion. She does it every day. Self-care does not have to be complicated. In fact, the simpler it is, the more likely it is that you will do it. Figure out what works for you.

Some notes about the time definitions:

- These are only suggestions. If you want to give yourself a hand massage for an hour – *do it!* If you can feel the benefits of a bath in fifteen minutes, *do it!*
- You can mix and match times to build a longer stretch of self-care. Say you have three hours. You could take a bath (thirty minutes) and do a mani/ pedi (two hours) and a facial (thirty minutes). Or you could go get a massage (three hours).
- If you want a truly guided experience, use the activities from the book in order and keep moving forward!
- Anything in the "Ongoing" section (Chapter 16) can be used at any time, so check it out and see if you want to try any of those for your daily allotment of self-care time.
- Some of the times may seem inflated – that is to account for travel/ drive time. I know how it works if you only set aside an hour for a massage. You race to get there, have the massage feeling a little stressed because you are taking so much time out of your day, then race back to life. Instead, plan for three hours. Much better. You can even stop for coffee or tea afterward if you want.

Some of the ideas in the following chapters may not currently be available due to the pandemic. *(Won't that sentence be weird to read in our future post-pandemic world? "Hey! We made it!")* I am including them anyway because some day, the world will be open again. It might take you a while to work up to a whole weekend of self-care!

The end goal here is to condition yourself to require self-care as a consistent practice. If you follow the guidance in this book, it will happen.

Tips:

✓ Journal so you notice your growth. There are a lot of apps for this type of journaling, but you can also use a notebook. Nothing fancy – spend about five minutes in the morning setting your intention (*not* a to-do list, but something like "I will really disconnect from my responsibilities for five [or fifteen, or thirty, or whatever number] minutes today") and five minutes in the evening noticing the effects of your intention. If your reflection is that you forgot you even set an intention... so what? Do it again the next day. We are building something new here. Again, did you walk without falling the first time? Nope.

✓ Keep track of your progress. I have created a really basic tracking sheet at the end of this book. There's a free printable version on my website (https://yourapocalypse.com) You can also look for an app that works or use your journal.

✓ Celebrate your achievements. Your celebration does not have to be champagne (but it can be!). It can be a pat on the back, a mini dance party, some kind words to yourself... but do something! When you twitch your way through five minutes but you finish it – *celebrate*! When you manage a thirty-minute spot of self-care – *celebrate*! All the things – celebrate yourself. I'll go into this in more detail in Chapter 8.

✓ If you miss a few days, no biggie. Start again using the amount of time you were using one step earlier. So if you get up to thirty minutes a day of self-care and you skip a day or three, go back to fifteen minutes and work that fifteen-minute muscle more.

✓ Set some personal goals. Here are some examples:

- "I will enjoy an uninterrupted hour of self-care unapologetically by [DATE]."
- "I will lavish myself in self-care for a minimum of fifteen minutes/ day for thirty days straight starting [DATE]."
- "I will spend one half-day per month dedicated only to my self-care for the entire year of 20XX."

Then plan accordingly. Remember, if it is not scheduled, it will not happen.

✓ Invite a friend or family member to join you on this journey. Accountability has never hurt anyone. You know yourself and what kind of accountability helps you. Use it. And if you convince a friend to prioritize their self-care, you're helping someone else too!

✓ Connect to your why and enhance it as needed.

✓ Do the challenge at the end of the book.

———

✎ Some of the activities above need to be set up before you start. Go ahead and take some time to do that now.

———

Alrighty! Let's do this!

8

FIVE MINUTES

*Y*ou'll probably notice that many of the items in this chapter can be done in a moment. Take your time. Do not rush. Take the full five minutes for yourself. Mix and match a couple or even a few if you need to, or just relax for the remainder of the time after you finish the activity you've chosen for the day.

ASK FOR HELP

Let me tell you a tale of the woman who never asked for help. Okay, the whole tale would take way too long, so I will just share a chapter from that story.

(The woman is me, in case you didn't guess.)

I think it was 2014. I was scheduled for back surgery after years of all the other things I had done in an attempt to alleviate back pain. The recovery time would be at least six weeks. My daughters were ten and four. My husband worked nights.

In the months leading up to the surgery date, I had three

friends who fairly consistently asked how they could help me during my recovery.

They all had families and jobs and their own lives. I did not want to impose. So each time, I would politely decline... brush it off... tell them I would let them know.

... That is, until about a week before the surgery, when I realized my kids still needed to eat and it might be kind of nice to have some help with that. My dad was coming up for the two weeks immediately following the surgery and could definitely provide meals, but I went ahead and texted my friends anyway, something simple like "Hi – if you are still interested in helping, we could use some dinners... I would really appreciate it!" It took all of twenty seconds.

They all responded quickly and were happy to be of service. I think they each ended up bringing two or three meals – all enough for leftovers. It was wonderful.

We like to help other people. It makes us feel good. When I did not accept my friends' offers of help, I was actually denying them good feelings.

Ask for help. That will come up in your self-care, especially if you have children. You are probably going to have to either ask the kids to help you by letting you have time or ask another adult if the kids are too young to manage the length of time you need.

As an aside, it is totally fine to plop your kids in front of a movie (or two, in some instances) so you can care for yourself. Let them play movie theater.

Remember that.

CHECK YOUR MEANING

"Nothing has any meaning beyond the meaning we give it."

That was a life-changing statement for me. I learned it

when I was going through training to get my current coaching job.

We give everything meaning. Sometimes, that meaning is accurate. Sometimes, it is not.

I will give an example.

My daughter had some friends over to have a cake-baking contest. She promised they would clean everything up. I knew our ideas of clean were different, but when I walked into the kitchen after they'd left, I felt my blood boil.

It looked like cakes had exploded all over the kitchen. I was livid. I immediately had some very unflattering thoughts about the kids – including my daughter.

I assigned the meaning that they were thoughtless, selfish, obnoxious kids who did not have to be responsible for anything, so they did not care about my space.

I texted my daughter and made it *very* clear that she was to come home alone and clean the kitchen.

What happened was that three of the kids came back with her. I heard them and went down to the kitchen to send them away, still angry.

What I saw was four terrified kids frantically cleaning a kitchen. Thank *gawd* I knew about assigning meaning. They all stopped, froze, and looked at me with desperation on their faces.

One of them, a boy, squeaked out, "I tried to tell her we needed to clean it, but she said you'd be cool about it if she cleaned it later."

I almost laughed out loud. Then I did laugh. I looked at my daughter – she was nodding. She told me they all tried to convince her to clean before they left.

Granted, better communication should have happened, but it was a great teachable moment. I told them exactly that. I asked how their parents would have felt if they had been in my shoes. I shared my point of view and how, if I had known they planned to clean up later, everything would have been cool and they wouldn't have been standing in my kitchen afraid of me.

Nothing has any meaning but the meaning you give it. I could have saved myself some rage energy if I had checked the meaning. All you must do is ask yourself, "Is that real?" And then be honest.

EXPAND YOUR EMOTIONAL VOCABULARY

Did you know there are hundreds, if not thousands, of words that describe different emotions?

Humans use about twelve regularly.

Who cares?

You should, and here's why: we give meaning with words. If you want to feel more things, you must use more words.

Earlier I mentioned a coaching exercise I went through early on – picking an emotion I wanted to feel. Part of my struggle at the time was that my emotional vocabulary was thin. I did not know many words to describe my feelings.

I would have passed out in embarrassment to use the word "ecstasy" back then. So I never felt it.

Now, bring it on.

We tell our brain how we feel using words. The idea is to learn enough words to describe various emotions that you can minimize negative feelings and enhance positive feelings.

Instead of "pissed," maybe you are "perturbed." Instead of "okay," maybe you are feeling "even-keeled." Instead of "happy," maybe you are "joyous." "Angry"? Maybe "agitated." "Exhausted"? Maybe "low energy."

Once you get good at this, you will be ecstatic too!

HAND MASSAGE

I always thought it was so weird in TV shows and movies when the woman/ wife would put lotion on her hands before bed. I had to wonder if everyone else did that. I still wonder that.

Anyway, here's the dealio on this one: any lotion will do, but if you pick a lotion that feels and smells luxurious to you, winner winner chicken dinner!

Don't be shy about this. Dig right in! Your hands are full of pressure points and you will be surprised by how much tension is in your digits. Feel free to include your wrists and forearms.

I remember when I was about ten-million years pregnant with my second daughter, I was at the mall for some reason. I was aimlessly wandering (I may have been lost... who knows?) when an Aveda employee stepped out of the salon and offered a hand massage. I had not indulged in that previously, so I figured, why not?

I fell asleep with my head on the table. Probably snored. Possibly drooled. I still think she was so kind to ignore that.

FOOT MASSAGE

Like the hand massage – a sweet smelling lotion is nice.

While it is a nice thing to get a foot rub from someone else, it is surprisingly luxurious to give yourself one. Notice how enjoyable it is – especially since you know your own tickle-spots!

Pay attention to your tootsies. Every toe needs some love! Spend time where your feet need it the most – they will tell you. Ankles and shins/ calves are a great place to use residual lotion.

If you want to up your game, look up pressure points on

the internet. Pressure points are magical spots that affect your body and health more than other non-magical spots on your body. Give it a try – you won't regret it!

FOOT SOAK

I love this one! Well, I love them all... but this one is surprisingly a lot of bang for your buck, time-wise.

Leave your phone on the counter – this is not time to surf social media! Light a candle if you'd like.

Grab a cushion or folded towel and sit on it on the edge of your tub. (If you do not have a tub, a big bowl or pot will do!)

Fill the tub/ container with enough water to cover your ankles, as hot as you like it.

Soak. Feel your muscles relaxing. Listen to the swooshing of the water as you move your feet.

Bonus points for adding essential oils or Epsom salt to this experience. If you are really feeling luxurious, follow up with a foot massage. (See what I did there?)

LEAVE THE DISHES

I spent years battling what seemed like the entire universe regarding dishes in the sink. I could not understand how someone could not quite make the two-foot move from the sink to the dishwasher.

Stress, frustration, irritation, resignation... the feeling of being disrespected... I gave this situation so much meaning.

Until I did not.

One night, I left the dishes in the sink so I could enjoy time with my kids without extending everyone's bedtime. (I will be honest, this was with coaching help.)

You know what happened?

I relaxed. I laughed with my kids. We all got to bed on time.

The dishes were still dirty in the morning. It was fine.

If you're thinking, "But I can't relax if the kitchen isn't clean!" or "I hate starting the morning with a mess first thing," I understand. I used to be that way. And, for the most part, I still clean up at night or as I go.

But allowing the option of leaving the dishes is more life-changing than you would think.

Leave the dishes in the kitchen and out of your mind.

ORACLE CARDS

I personally love my cards. I have all sorts: Angel, Nature, Tarot, Ascended Master, Manifestation… I really enjoy them.

If you're new to the cards, basically you focus on an intention or a question and draw a card. Whatever's on the card usually provides some clarity.

I use mine mostly when I need to get centered or grounded about something. It gives me time to clear my mind and think about what I really want to know or where I'm feeling stuck. I go through phases during which I'll pull a card or three each morning.

For the sake of this book, check out self-care Oracle cards. There are a number of decks to choose from – I even made one to go along with this book. You can take a look at it on my website (https://yourapocalypse.com). If you have a self-care deck, you can use it when you're low on ideas.

LAUGHTER YOGA

Yep, it's a thing. A quick Google search will return several five-minute (or shorter!) "Intro to Laughter Yoga" videos. You can also do longer sessions when you have more time.

If you cannot find a way to add laughter yoga into your life, I am not sure what to think other than please, please, please give yourself permission to take care of yourself!

It is silly. It is fun. Laughter creates endorphins. And you can do it in five minutes or less!

Think about how great you feel after a good belly laugh. How about when you can't quite breathe and your laugh is so hard it is silent? What about when tears fall down your face? Ever let one of those snorts out?

You can usually count on me for a snort and a solid gasp for air.

I love laughing.

ESSENTIAL OILS

Oooooohhhhh, so much to do with these! You may have a favorite or you may have never smelled an essential oil in your life. This is wonderful either way.

Some studies have shown benefits related to specific oils. Scent is such a personal thing that you'll have to choose your personal favorite oils for yourself, but here's a little bit of info to get you started finding oils that will benefit you.

- Reduce stress/ anxiety: bergamot, cedarwood, cinnamon, citronella, jasmine, lemongrass, neroli, rose
- Energize: grapefruit, lemon, orange
- Enhance mood: basil, helichrysum, lemon, orange
- Increased focus: rosemary
- Relaxation: lavender, patchouli, sandalwood

This particular activity combines essential oil with breathwork.

When we are stressed, frustrated, or overwhelmed, we

forget how to breathe. I mean, we don't die... but we do not access our full capabilities on the breathing front.

Grab your favorite essential oil. This might change based on the season or your mood! Put a drop or two on your palm. Rub your hands together and then cup them over your nose and mouth.

Close your eyes.

Breathe in for the count of four. Hold for the count of seven. Breathe out for the count of eight.

Repeat for five minutes.

Disclaimer: Some oils are not recommended for pregnant women – please do your research!

RETURN TO SENDER

If you pay attention to your thoughts, you will start to notice repeat visitors. When these visitors are not friendly, they are not welcome.

When you have a thought that is unkind toward yourself, it probably did not come from you originally. You may or may not know how it started, but that is not really important for this exercise.

How it works is, when you notice a thought that does not serve you, simply say, "Return to sender."

You may say it out loud or in your head. You might add "with love"... or maybe not. Either way, the thought that doesn't serve you is not yours, so do not keep it.

Return to sender.

DECIDE

We all have at least one of those things we've been thinking about it for a while, bouncing choices around in our heads. This one... no, that one... no, this one. *What if I'm wrong?*

Ask a different question. What if you are right?

I'll share a story. One of my clients had been agonizing over setting a wedding date for quite some time. When we dug just a little, it turned out she had already made a decision: she knew that to marry the person she was engaged to would be a mistake. As soon as she acknowledged that, the decision about wedding dates fell away. The real choice was about staying with someone she knew she didn't really love, and it was actually a very simple decision that she had already made in her heart.

Here's a tip, though. I got this from Tony Robbins, and it is the simplest thing. Two options are a dilemma. If you are attempting a decision and you only have two options, you will be locked in a battle with yourself for quite a while.

Instead, come up with a third option. Get out of your head.

Then make the decision.

In the example I shared above, initially my client's options were to set a date or delay the wedding. When asked to think of a third choice, she came up with ending the engagement. In a matter of moments, she chose to end the engagement, and then we began the work on how to go about that.

You may not have scheduled time to act on the decision immediately. I get that. Simply make the decision.

You'll feel better.

GET UP AND MOVE

Walk, run, jog, dance, wiggle... just do something. When you have a strong self-care game, this will probably become part of your regular daily routine.

I heard somewhere that if we sit and stare at something for longer than fifteen minutes, our brain slips into predator mode and we can't focus as well on what we are doing. We actually stop using our peripheral vision! I have not scientifically verified this, but it makes sense.

I remember when I first heard this idea, my initial reaction was, "Well, that is irrelevant to me – I never stare at anything that long."

… unless it is a computer screen. How about you?

Get up and shake that ass!

CLEAR YOUR ENERGY

I keep palo santo sticks all over my house. Incense works as well, or you can mix lavender essential oil with water in a spray bottle.

If I am feeling a little off or "ishy" (or sometimes just to be proactive), I will light my palo santo stick and "douse" myself. Sage works too. Dousing means that I get the smoke on me.

Fresh air and sunlight are wonderful for clearing energy as well.

Whatever your pleasure is, go for it!

ONE-SONG DANCE PARTY

So simple!

Even if you are not in the mood to dance, changing your physiology is the number one simplest way to change your mood.

Pick a song.

Dance like nobody's watching.

If you still have time in your five minutes, repeat.

CELEBRATE YOU!

One of the ways we can anchor our progress is by actually noticing it.

We often miss our own growth because we are so hard on ourselves and we are consistently looking to do better.

We can do better for ourselves by taking the time to notice the small steps that lead us to the huge leaps.

So how can you celebrate? You could do a quick dance party for yourself. You could lift your hand up over your head and reach back and pat yourself on the back. You could make yourself a sticker chart and pick some pretty, sparkly stickers. You could look in the mirror and tell yourself, "You are *amazing!*"

Celebration can be so simple, and the impact will train your brain to notice your awesomeness more.

And who among us couldn't use more of that?

By the way, you freakin' rock!!

LOVE NOTES TO YOU

Grab a pen and some sticky notes or index cards. You can use markers or colored pencils or plain old pen and paper. Be as fancy as you want or as plain as you'd like.

Write yourself some short and quick love notes.

You can be serious or silly, but make it fun. The notes can say anything from "Well, hello Queen!!!" to "I love the way you keep trying until you make it work. Keep going!" to "Your eyes make me smile."

If it is difficult for you to write these notes to yourself, imagine you are writing them to someone else. But write at least twenty!

When you are done, hide the notes for your future self to find. Yeah, you will know where some of them are, but you will not find them all right away. Tuck them in books... in drawers... in pockets of your winter coats... in the glove box of your car... you get it! If you live with someone, you could add some notes for them. So fun!

Future You will smile. I know she will.

QUICK FOAM ROLL

I don't know how I lived life before I got my foam roller. Okay – that's not completely true. I was young and supple!

If you do not have a foam roller, I highly recommend you invest in one.

If you do have one, use it.

Sit for a moment with your eyes closed and relax your body. Find your tension.

Roll it out.

YouTube is great for how-to videos!

REBOUNDER/ MINI-TRAMPOLINE

There are many health benefits to using one of these regularly. I will not go into all of them here.

What I will say is that a rebounder can improve your emotional state in five minutes. How can you jump up and down for five minutes and not feel better?

You won't even get sweaty in five minutes. Well, you won't get *that* sweaty. (What am I even saying? Maybe you are sweatier than I am. Or maybe you work harder on the rebounder.)

Regardless, start jumping! You won't regret it.

SUN/ AIR ON YOUR SKIN

The simplicity of this one almost takes my breath away.

Go outside, no matter the weather. You can take an umbrella if you need to.

Feel the outside. You can close your eyes – or not – whichever feels right.

The heat of the sun on your back or face, or wherever you feel like having it.

The air – whatever temperature – on your skin.

Breathe in through your nose and out through your mouth, taking a count of five for each.

Notice the smells and sounds.

That is it.

SING LIKE A STAR

This one is versatile.

You can do it in your car (with the windows down if you are really feeling brave). Add a little seat dance to it for extra results.

You can grab the TV remote and be the performer of your dreams in your living room.

You can do it in the shower.

The only rule is that you must do it loudly. Who cares how it sounds? It feels good!

JUMPING JACKS

Okay, five minutes of jumping jacks is a lot.

And, if I am honest, boobs. I don't have a strong enough bra for five minutes of jumping jacks!

But the idea is to change your physiology.

I like to mix jumping jacks up with the Wonder Woman

pose. Standing in that pose for three to five minutes has been proven to raise confidence. It feels good and is great for your posture. Add in breathwork by breathing deep into your belly while holding the pose. You can even breathe in through your nose and out through your mouth.

If you don't know what the Wonder Woman pose is (it's also called the superhero pose, to be inclusive!), the internet is your friend.

I will usually do ten to thirty jumping jacks and then Wonder Woman pose (breathwork included) for about four minutes and finish with more jumping jacks. Play some music. Trust me.

———

✎ Where will you begin? Pick the first three activities you want to do and get them scheduled in your calendar. Do it. Trust me.

———

9

FIFTEEN MINUTES

SKINCARE ROUTINE

I cannot even tell you how many different fancy skin products I have invested in over the years. More annoying than how much I've spent is how much I've wasted.

My pattern was starting strong and fading away... until I finally cracked the code.

As much as rushing through smearing lotion or cream or serum on my face just to say I had done it sounds appealing, it does not have any staying power as a routine. Anyone relate?

Here's the answer: treat your skin like you love it.

You don't need fancy products. But you do need intention and care... and sunscreen. That's important!

Whatever products you use, take some time to appreciate your skin.

Massage your moisturizer into your face and body. Allow time for your skin to absorb it. Listen to a podcast or music.

Make it an experience. Your skin is your largest organ. Treat it accordingly.

SPEED TIDY

YESSSSS! While I may not always love cleaning, doing a quick tidy in a short amount of time gets great results.

I admit that I sometimes still tell myself I must be in the right mood to clean or tidy up. But I can do anything for fifteen minutes!

Pick something that needs a little clean-up, maybe an area you have been avoiding. Set your timer and *go to it!* See how much you can get done.

I keep baskets on the stairs for just this reason. I do not need to waste my valuable speed-tidying time going up and down stairs! (Though if you want to add some challenge to your life, this is a good cardio workout!)

When the timer goes off, you are done! Stand back and admire your work.

ACKNOWLEDGE THE MISTAKE/ GIVE THE APOLOGY

If there is something you are feeling guilty or remorseful about, you can say so. Likewise, if you make a mistake, the quickest path to relief is to admit it.

Apologizing or admitting a mistake does not mean you are wrong or bad or suck as a human.

It means you recognize you caused some sort of damage, you feel badly about it, and you are working to change your behavior. And you may need some help doing that.

It is important to include yourself here. Is there anything for which you could apologize to yourself?

EAT A TREAT

This is another one that requires the phone to be out of reach. Do not multitask.

Find a cozy spot. Light a candle. Play some music.

Create a sensual experience.

What is visually appealing? What does the smell remind you of? What is it about the texture that you enjoy? How do the tastes mix to create magic in your mouth?

Eat your decadent treat one bite at a time. Put the fork or treat down between bites. Do not take another bite until you have swallowed the previous one.

Savor the experience.

STRETCH SESSION

Mmmmmmm, stretching.

You know that first stretch of the morning? The one you do automatically? The one that feels *soooooo* good?

You can do that any time! For reals!

I have done enough physical therapy and had enough bodywork done over the years that I have a library of stretches in my brain, but I also *love* YouTube for this. You can search for general stretches, or, if you've got a particular body-part that's bugging you, search for that. And, once you find some you like, make a playlist.

Been sitting at your computer for a while? How about some neck and shoulder stretches, or a hip flexor stretch?

Lower back pain? Maybe your glutes need some stretching. Could be your hamstrings are tight.

Listen to your body and give it some stretching.

RESTORATIVE YOGA

You may remember that I admitted to being too impatient to do yoga earlier in the book. Well, a back surgery and some wisdom later… I learned.

I started with restorative (or Yin) yoga. What I like about this style of yoga is that I do not have to think so much about keeping up with the instructor because it is slower-paced and the poses are held for longer.

I love it. It is awesome before bed, or any time you could use some calm.

If you are new to yoga, YouTube again. I am a huge fan of SarahBethYoga.

QI GONG

Translated, this means "vital energy cultivation." It is like moving meditation – it combines gentle movement, getting your energy flowing, and breathwork.

Qi gong is probably my new favorite thing. There is nothing new about it though. It's been around for thousands of years.

I've sent my dad some YouTube videos about qi gong. I am telling all my clients about it. I tried to convince my sister to do it in her RV.

With how much I talk about it, you'd think I invented it.

I am such a huge believer in energy work, and qi gong is fantastic. It is easy and it feels amazing. You can feel your energy zinging through your body after you have done a session.

It feels like you are a statue coming to life, from stone to flesh and blood.

How can you learn more? You guessed it – YouTube.

Personally, I have a morning routine and an evening routine saved in my YouTube library.

TAI CHI

Now, this is what you see in movies with old people on the grass in a park moving very slowly. Can you imagine it?

Well, tai chi is not just for old people. When you are bored with your workout routine, toss a little tai chi into your day.

Movement is crucial for our health and, though this isn't fast sweaty movement, it is wonderful. It builds up your mindfulness, too.

Head to YouTube!

LEGS-UP WALL POSE

There are a range of benefits to doing this pose.

Just to name a few: it helps with blood flow and digestion. It's an amazing stretch for your lower back and hamstrings. It decreases any swelling/ bloating in your feet and legs.

… and it is super relaxing. It would be really boring to watch a YouTube video of this one, so here is how you do it:

1. Sit down facing the wall
2. Lie back and lift your legs up
3. Scooch your butt closer and closer to the wall (think OB-GYN scooch) until your butt is up against the wall and your legs are straight up
4. Enjoy for fifteen minutes (or longer if you want)

I sometimes meditate in this position. Other times I do it while I am watching Netflix. It depends on my mood!

TAPPING

Tapping is another name for Emotional Freedom Technique. If you have never experienced it, you are in for a treat.

According to The Tapping Solution, which is both a website and an app you can download onto your device (I definitely recommend it!), "Tapping is a combination of ancient Chinese acupressure and modern psychology that works to physically alter your brain, energy system, and body all at once. The practice consists of tapping with your fingertips on specific meridian points while talking through traumatic memories and a wide range of emotions."

In plain speak, it makes you feel better even though you don't really know why. If you are an experienced tapper, remember to add this into your self-care library. If you are not, check out The Tapping Solution. You can use the free/lite version to get into the practice of it. There is enough available for free for you to add this to your toolkit right away. If you find you enjoy it, there is a version for purchase.

… Or there is always YouTube.

———

✎ Pick one, two, or even three of these activities and – yep, you got it – mark your calendar. If you need to go out a week or two, feel free.

———

THIRTY MINUTES

TAKE A BATH

*D*raw yourself a bath, *daaaahhling*.

I'm talking essential oil, Epsom salt, candles, and wine (if you are so inclined). Invest in a tub pillow. If you do not have one, a rolled-up towel will do in a pinch.

You can do this in the middle of the day. You can do it early in the morning. You can do it after the kids go to bed. That is the cool thing about being an adult woman: you can choose when to take a bath.

Close (and if possible, lock) the door. Light your candle(s). Turn the lights off. Sink into the blissfully steamy water, lie back, and relax.

Baths are a great opportunity to meditate or listen to music, or even catch an episode on Netflix.

I used to have the *best* soaking tub. It was fabulous. I moved into a rental and the bathtub isn't nearly as big and, so far, I haven't found a plug that works for longer than five minutes. But I still enjoy a bath every now and then! Do not use your tub as an excuse not to take a bath. It is all about your mindset.

MAKE AND ENJOY YOUR TEA/ COFFEE/ COCKTAIL

Remember when you ate your treat? This is along the same lines.

The point of this activity is to fully experience your drink.

For hot drinks, listen to the sound of the coffee percolating or the water boiling. Smell the aroma as it wafts through the air. Breathe in the scent of the tea bag. If you use milk or cream, watch as it swirls into the hot beverage.

If you are making your favorite cocktail, pay attention to how the liquids look and mix. Notice any effervescence. Listen to any sounds. Feel the fizz on your lips. Is the ice clear or foggy?How does it clink in the glass?

If soda (or pop or coke, depending on where you live) is your thing, listen to the *pffffft* of the container opening. Hear the bubbles and the ice. Pour the drink slowly into the glass. See if you can manage the foam. Watch as the carbonation settles.

Whatever your beverage, sit down in a cozy spot to enjoy it. Savor it. No gulping allowed.

LIGHT THERAPY

You may want to do your own research on this one, but it can really be helpful when used appropriately.

We need a certain amount of sunlight to be healthy. The sun helps us with our vitamin D and serotonin (happy/ calm hormones). When we do not get enough exposure to the sun, we can fake it to a certain extent by using special light therapy. What I'm talking about here is at-home light therapy with a special lamp (Google to find one).

I am in Minnesota and it gets dark very early here in the winter months. There's not much daylight to take advantage of. I, personally, do not suffer from seasonal affective disorder (also known as seasonal depression) but I know many people who do and many of them use light therapy. My daughter uses her light lamp starting in late fall and all through winter and she says it helps.

TRY A NEW MORNING BEVERAGE

Switch up your morning drink. There are many options that are healthy and, usually, tasty!

Here are some ideas:

- Chicory
- Golden milk
- Matcha tea
- Lemon water
- Yerba mate
- Chai
- Rooibos

Check out the previous idea (Make and Enjoy Your Tea/ Coffee/ Cocktail) and focus on fully experiencing your drink. Tap into every sense you can.

If you are feeling adventurous, give these two a try:

- Kombucha
- Apple cider vinegar (hold your nose!). You can mix this or take it plain – you're the boss here. One to two tablespoons is plenty!

FACE MASQUE*

Mask" works, but since I'm not trying to tell you to put on your pandemic face mask and relax, I opted for "masque."

Remember loving your skin? This is another chance to do just that!

Step 1: Pick out a face masque. There are a variety to choose from: bubbly, warm, tingly, clay, mud, cooling, moisturizing, toning, cleansing… and even more!

Step 2: Prepare your space for relaxation. I like to snuggle into my bedroom and catch an episode of whatever series I am into, or sometimes I call my sister.

Step 3: Wash your face.

Step 4: Put the masque on and relax for fifteen minutes or so, per instructions.

Step 5: Rinse/ remove the masque and flow right into your skincare routine. *So delicious for your skin*!

WATCH THE SUNRISE/ SUNSET

When is the last time you just sat and enjoyed the sky? I absolutely love the sky. The clouds… the color… the bigness… I *love* the sky.

My kids laugh at me because I get so excited about a sunset. Or a cloud. Or the moon.

It always feels new to me.

If you have a good view from your house, that's cool… but you still must create an experience.

Pick your beverage of choice, maybe a decadent snack if you are so inclined, find a comfortable place to sit, and take it all in. Notice everything you can. Involve your senses.

If you need to drive to find a good view, do that. I have had some enjoyable experiences sitting in my parked car focusing on the sunset. You can also take a chair or blanket and a little picnic if that is an option. If you choose to go that route, you may need to block out more time on your calendar for this one.

DAYDREAM

I find myself doing this more these days. My calendar is probably the least cluttered it has ever been.

I will catch myself standing in the middle of the room not quite sure what to do. These moments are not quite like when you get to a room and you forget why you are there (though I do that too). When I notice I am doing this, I find a comfy place to sit and allow myself to daydream. Sometimes I stare out a window. Sometimes I pet the cat.

I notice all sorts of things that I never pay attention to. Do you have any idea how much cat hair can get stuck on the leg of a couch?

I do not usually think about anything in an organized way. If my mind tries to latch on to something that does not feel good, I shake my head and take a really deep breath. That usually does the trick.

I get some cool ideas and I always feel quite relaxed afterward.

Give it a whirl. You might like it.

WATCH AN EPISODE OF YOUR FAVORITE SHOW

I do this when I eat lunch. (And I take a break to eat lunch – hint, hint. Not at my desk.)

I look forward to it. It is a real break.

It is a real break *whenever* you do it. That is the cool part. You can do it during the day. In the morning. In the afternoon. Whenever!

Totally relax into it. You do not have to set an alarm,

because you know that when the episode is over, your break is over.

You can lose yourself in the show, and I recommend that you do.

PLAN A PITY PARTY

If you are having some trouble feeling stuck in a sorry-for-yourself state of mind, plan a pity party. Look at your calendar and schedule thirty minutes to just wallow in all your poor-me glory.

Then, any time you start to revisit that feeling before your formally scheduled time, just remember you have a whole party set up – coming soon!

More often than not, your pity party reminder will pop up and you will not even need to feel sorry for yourself. You just gained thirty minutes to do whatever you please!

Or you can feel sorry for yourself.

You choose.

LISTEN TO YOUR FAVORITE PODCAST

Have you ever noticed how, when you are listening to a podcast/ audiobook while doing something else, you miss a lot of the words?

Me too! But I still do it sometimes. That is not the purpose of this activity.

For this one, you are only listening. Not emailing... not doing laundry... not cooking... just listening.

You could have a beverage or snack. You could take notes if you want.

Whatever enhances the listening experience is allowed.

GO TO A PARK AND SWING

In all honesty, this one makes me nauseous, which is kind of a bummer because I love the sensation of swinging... until I feel like I am going to hurl chunks.

If that does not happen to you, give this one a shot. Play is one of the best forms of self-care.

If there is a park in walking distance, all the better. Enjoy the walk – it is like a double-batch of fun!

Hop on the swing and just relax into the up-and-down and back-and-forth feeling.

Don't be afraid to laugh out loud. I do!

BRAINSTORM A PROBLEM

I love, love, love brainstorming.

Here is the dealio on it: you can't use judgment. *What?* That's right, to successfully brainstorm, you do not judge your ideas. It is judgment-free.

See, our habit is to try and figure out *how* to do things. The "how" often locks us up. So let's leave that alone at first.

Think of a problem you have been struggling to solve – or, more likely, avoiding. Think about how you'd feel on the other side of it, once you've come up with the solution. That is the feeling you want to grab on to. Really soak that up.

Then, write down everything you can think of that would help solve the problem. The ideas can be ridiculous, far-fetched, seemingly impossible. Write them down anyway. Get the mind going. If you allow it, you will figure it out. There is something about writing things down that makes a huge difference.

Once you have a nice long list, put it aside for a day or so. Your mind will keep going on it. See what comes up.

This is a fun activity to do with a friend or close family member. More brains.

DO YOUR FAVORITE WORKOUT

This one is so simple.

Just do it. Without apology.

TRY A NEW WORKOUT FROM YOUR LIVING ROOM

This may take some research, but maybe not. It could be you have been eyeing that belly dance class online for a while. What do I know?

Find something that you have never done before and do it. You do not have to do it well. You do not even have to do it thoroughly. But do not quit before it is over, unless you really can't stand it. (Self-care is trial and error sometimes.)

Trying new workouts is a great way to build your self-care toolbox. I will probably never have a Brazilian booty, but I definitely have the option to add the variety to my workout.

I have found that I consistently work out when I do not get bored with my workouts. (Don't get me wrong, I am not an every-day-no-matter-what-I-gotta-sweat person, but I do something that gets me moving every day.)

Here is a list of the different movement/ exercises I still do (every now and then) because I tried them once or twice over the years:

- Weighted hula-hooping
- Body Groove
- Kundalini yoga
- Qi gong
- Tai chi
- Svelte Training

- Yin yoga
- Weightlifting
- Jumping rope
- Belly dancing (I am so awkward at this!)
- Egoscue

Feel free to give 'em a try! You'll notice a few of them are listed in other sections – that's how much I love them!

———

✍ I bet you're catching on – it's time to schedule something. Choose the activity that seems the most awesome for you. I challenge you to get this one on the calendar within two weeks.

———

ONE HOUR

MANICURE OR PEDICURE

*Y*ou do not have to wear fancy color on your nails to enjoy a manicure or pedicure.

Go for the whole experience: soak, exfoliate, moisturize, massage, trim, file, and then paint if you want to.

Enjoy yourself. A warm soak followed by a moisturizing massage can be so relaxing.

Indulge yourself.

(The reason this is listed as an either/ or option for an hour is so you have time to relax while your nails dry if you do paint them.)

READ FOR PLEASURE

Going along with the idea that we must be producing something to be of value (*false!*), we were somehow conditioned to focus our reading on topics that teach us or make us better people.

That is awesome. I am all for learning and growing.

But every now and then, there is nothing wrong with picking up a romance novel, mystery, or sci-fi adventure story if that is your thing.

In my opinion, there is nothing wrong with spending most of your reading time reading for pure enjoyment. Let's be real – it is not a bad way to escape the stress of our world!

Go ahead. Grab that trashy novel and dig in!

WALKING MEDITATION: SEE/ HEAR/ SMELL

My daughter just told me she cannot meditate because she cannot focus long enough to clear her mind.

I will tell you what I think, since she does not really want to hear me espouse the benefits of meditation.

Meditation is not a blank mind. I would never do it if that were true! I mean, some people are interested in that, I suppose. But not me.

It is also not about focus.

Meditation is about being present and allowing yourself to observe thoughts without latching on to them and chewing them to a pulp to solve all your problems.

That is why I love walking meditation. It is basically a walk during which you notice things outside. By doing that, your thoughts do not win the day.

Notice the colors and sounds and smells... or pick just one at a time to really pay attention to.

You will be surprised by what you discover all around you.

WRITE A THANK YOU LETTER TO YOUR YOUNGER SELF

Sometimes we hold on to feelings about ourselves that do not serve us. I know I made decisions when I was younger that I certainly would not make now. I can look back on my life and see times when I behaved in ways that used to make me ashamed. I know I hurt people and let people down.

It is one thing to say and know that when we know better, we do better. That can help. But writing a letter to that version of myself was cathartic in a way that logical knowledge is not.

Any time you hold some resentment or shame toward yourself, find the root of that. You can probably write a letter to that version of you. We must forgive ourselves to be whole. Gratitude and forgiveness are powerful tools you can use on yourself.

Think back to a period in your life when you could have used a love letter.

Be the person to write that letter and show gratitude to your younger self.

WRITE A THANK YOU LETTER TO SOMEONE ELSE

This one can be very cathartic, or it can simply be a thank you. I have done it both ways.

You can write a letter you know you will send, or one you know you will not.

I have written to my exes, knowing I would not send those letters, to get from a negative place to one of gratitude and transmute it into peace. I did this just for me, voicing my anger and hurt.

I once wrote to a former lover to let him know he helped me know what it means to be loved for exactly who I am. I have no idea if he ever got the letter, because I sent it to his last known address and I do not know if he is even there anymore.

I have written to friends and to family. Some I sent, some I did not.

Sometimes, I will send a quick email when I have a feeling of gratitude and I can figure out who it is for.

A good way to know if you could use a dose of gratitude is if you have resentments toward someone. It may seem unpleasant at first to feel grateful for someone you're resenting, but what you resist can be a good indicator of work that needs doing.

Taking the time and effort to anchor your gratitude will make a difference in your life – and in the life of whomever the letter is written to, even if you do not mail it.

SET SOME GOALS

What would you do if there was nothing to stop you? Why aren't you doing it now?

If you do not think about this, you will not reach the goal. Our thoughts create our reality. If we cannot imagine something, we probably will not obtain it.

I have had a goal to write a book for over twenty years. This is the fifth one I have started and the first one I have finished. It is not like it just happened.

I had a goal to leave my corporate job. That *really* does not just happen.

Those are a couple of my huge goals. I also have smaller goals. It is the small goals that led to the giant, life-changing achievements. And trust me, my path has not been a straight line. I have faltered and failed and fallen flat on my face. But I keep finding something else to aim for.

Think about what you want. How do you want to feel?

Then think a little bigger, about a little more of that feeling. Even bigger, and even more.

There is nothing you can't do if you set your mind to it and have a strong enough purpose.

But you must have an outcome in mind so you can connect to it emotionally. That starts with goals.

STARGAZE

This one might require a drive if you live around city lights. It is worth it though.

Grab a blanket and your choice of beverage and lie down. It can be on the ground, on the hood of your car, in the back of your truck... just relax and use your peepers.If you want to really be luxurious (and why wouldn't you?), take a pillow and whatever else will make you super comfy.

How else will you be able to make that wish on a shooting star?

FANCY GROCERY STORE

I did this once by accident.

I cannot even remember the details of how I ended up at this particular store. I was not even grocery shopping that day. I think it was a co-op.

It was all organic, local, fancy stuff. I probably spent an hour just looking around. The store smelled healthy – in a good way.

My basket (one of the smaller ones, the kind you carry) was empty for most of the time because I was so curious about everything.

I ended up picking out a couple of new foods to try and a bottle of kombucha. It was delicious – both for my mouth and my soul.

DO A PUZZLE

I am not implying you can finish a puzzle in an hour. Or, maybe *you* can. Maybe you are a speed puzzler.

Is that a thing?

If not, you may need a place where you can leave an unfinished puzzle for this one.

I pulled a puzzle out earlier this year and it was super relaxing. I did not really care if I finished it, and – full disclosure – I never did.

But it was nice to just sit and work on it. It really clears the mind.

DECLUTTER A SPACE

We all have at least one of these spaces. Drawer, cabinet, shelf, table, bedroom, house (I jest)… whatever it is, it annoys you when you look at it.

Set your timer for an hour and get it done! Do not think, just do.

You can even use the Marie Kondo "spark joy" method. Touch everything only once…

1. Pick it up.
2. Does it spark joy?
3. Yes/ no
4. Put it where it goes it according to your answer.

I use a pretty simple sorting method: keep, toss, donate, or storage. I recently downsized, so not much gets stored, but every now and then, I will do that.

When you are finished, admire your work. *YASSSSSSSSSS!!*

MAKE A PLAYLIST: MUSIC/ YOGA/ MEDITATION

I love playlists. I have them for all my moods – so far. I am sure there will be more to come.

As you may have noticed, I am a heavy YouTube user. I do not use the paid version, and there's plenty of content, so *yay*!

YouTube is my go-to for yoga, stretches, new workouts, meditations... all the goodness. Anyway, whenever I find something I enjoy, it goes right into a playlist. I subscribe to the page where I found the video too, so I can peruse later.

I use Spotify for music, so that is where my music playlists are... and podcasts! *So* many yummy things for your ears.

While I do a lot of playlist-building as I go, I also enjoy sitting down with the intention to create something new and amazing. You can be general or very specific. For a long time, one of my favorite playlists was full of love songs that made me feel the way I want to feel in a relationship. I also have one that is just my favorite songs – no theme. You can do whatever you want!

Pick a mood or a topic and go for it! You will be glad you did.

TWO HOURS

SORT YOUR DRAWERS

*N*ot your underwear. (Or, yes, sure, if that is what you need to sort. Maybe you have an extensive collection of underwear.)

I mean dresser drawers.

Pull everything out. Make that giant pile on your bed. Then go through the pile piece by piece.

I have started making an effort not to keep things "just in case." If I have not worn something in a year, I probably do not love it. Also, shabby underwear has to go. You deserve nice underwear... even when you have your period. Same with holey socks – gotta go.

I always have my chosen receptacles ready:

- Plastic garbage bag for donation
- Bin for anything I am keeping but do not want in my drawer (like seasonal items)
- Paper bag for trash

If I am going to sell anything (and trust me, I do not usually make the effort), I will use plastic garbage bags with DONATE and SELL written on them in huge letters with Sharpie. I usually end up with far more DONATE bags than anything else.

Last, fold/ organize what is left and put it back in your drawers.

Admire your work. Nicely done.

BAKE SOMETHING

Baking can be so therapeutic. It is scientific, so you must be precise, unlike with cooking.

Measuring and mixing can really be meditative. It's a great chance to be present.

Either pick a favorite recipe or a brand new one. Taste the different flavors as you mix. Smell the aromas, notice the textures. Watch as the ingredients incorporate. Lick the spoon.

Enjoy the scent as your delicacy bakes. It is amazing how it changes form from liquid batter to a delicious treat.

When it is done, let it cool *just enough* for you to enjoy it warm. Find a nice spot to dig in and savor every moment.

MANI/ PEDI

This again! Only now you have *two whole hours* to yourself! Check the "One Hour" section (Chapter 11) if you want a refresher on how luxurious this should be. There's bound to be extra time here, so really enjoy yourself. Allow for all the time you need for your nails to dry before the next coat. Maybe add a foot and hand massage into the process.

Enjoy!

WATCH A MOVIE

Easy peasy!

Make some popcorn.

Grab some Milk Duds (or whatever your movie favorite is).

Get your favorite beverage.

Turn the lights off.

Cozy up in your ideal viewing spot and simply enjoy the whole movie!

TAKE YOUR FAVORITE MEAL AND MAKE IT SUPER HEALTHY

I have done this one many times.

Sometimes it turns out delicious… and sometimes it does not.

Once, my daughter told me her plate looked like a dog vomited on it. Ya win some, ya lose some.

The idea here isn't that you will end up with a masterpiece. The idea is that you get to have fun experimenting.

Take your favorite meal or recipe and see what you can swap out to make it healthier. What can you add? What could you eliminate?

I made muffins using bananas instead of eggs recently. After baking them for a gazillion minutes, I ended up having to microwave them and add butter to get my kids to eat them. They tasted like some sort of pudding cake. I invented a new thing, warm pudding cake with butter.

… sometimes we only use a recipe once.

GO SCREEN-FREE

This one can feel somewhat like a freefall from a plane. I do not know what it feels like to freefall from a plane, but you get my point. (As an aside, I do know what it feels like to freefall *in* a plane – I am a plane crash survivor! But that's another story for another day.)

Anyway, plan well, because you will twitch a little bit at first. You could go for a drive or a hike or a run or a nap (that's the next idea!) or try a combo of all of them as long as you aren't, say, napping and driving at the same time. Or you could do none of those things.

Maybe you will go through this book and build your own adventure. There are plenty of screen-free options!

You can do whatever you want, except for looking at a screen. Need help avoiding checking your phone for the full time? Set a timer!

NAP

I *love* naps. They are not just for babies and old people. (Well, my daughters consider me old, so... maybe they are.)

Make your bedroom as dark as you can. Maybe play some soft music. Sometimes I meditate. I have some good guided meditations saved because I know they put me to sleep.

Get into some comfy clothes.

Either get all the way under your covers or have a nice cozy blanket nearby in case you need it.

If you need to settle your mind, give breathwork a go. Breathe in for the count of four, hold it for the count of seven, breathe out for the count of eight. Do this a few times in a row and it will help you drift off.

Sweet dreams!

GET A THERAPIST

Okay, this one could take more than two hours if you do not have a therapist already.

My first therapist was in this really old two-story house in Minneapolis (that had been converted into offices – it's not like I was in someone's kitchen!). She charged on a sliding scale based on income and since I did not have an income, my dad would donate $10 or $20 to the cause for each appointment.

Since then, more insurance companies have decided that mental health matters and will cover some or all costs for therapy.

If you have insurance, check to see what they cover. If you do not have insurance, look for a therapist who uses a sliding scale – they're out there.

Another thing about this: you need a love match with your therapist. If you do not jive, pick a different one. You must be able to be completely open and vulnerable.

One of my favorite things I have ever heard a therapist say was, "I'm just the therapist before your next therapist." Leave a therapist if they are not helping.

TRY OUT A NATUROPATHIC DOCTOR

You may have noticed that I like information and learning. I am a very curious person. I also strongly believe in nature's ability to heal itself given the chance. We are made of nature.

So it makes sense to me to check out my options. I am an advocate for options. Western medicine has a purpose and is necessary, but, in my opinion, it is somewhat limited. When the pediatrician asks if I want them to give my daughter a fluoride treatment, it gives me pause. (I'm not sure why pediatricians even offer fluoride – the dentist handles that.)

Anyhoo, fluoride has been identified as a neurotoxin. I mean, it's in most of the public water here, so a fluoride treatment at the annual checkup isn't going to be the issue, but still.

So, other types of medicine. You can learn so much if you step outside your comfort zone. If you decide naturopathic medicine is not for you, at least you've made an educated decision.

See what's available to you and check it out. Note here: look for a *licensed* naturopathic doctor. They'll have "ND" or "NMD" after their name.

ORDER IN YOUR FAVORITE MEAL

A delicious meal with teeny-tiny effort.

Create a restaurant experience at home. Go for appetizers, an entrée, and even dessert! If drinks are on the menu, indulge.

You can set the table or get really comfy by eating *and* watching a movie at the same time. Or create a fine-dining situation, then move on to a movie or after-dinner cocktail. You're the boss!

Make it yummy!

PLAN YOUR DREAM VACATION – SKY'S THE LIMIT!

"Behave as if."

That is one of my favorite sentences. Behave as if you will be taking your dream vacation next year. It is time to plan!

Behave as if you have an unlimited budget.

Behave as if you have absolute control over your schedule.

Behave as if there is nothing in the way of you experiencing a vacation *exactly* as you want to.

Research locations, prices, options, and anything else you

need to end up with the perfect itinerary. If you really want an "as if" experience, you can mock up an actual itinerary or travel brochure.

Imagine yourself on the vacation. Close your eyes and see the sights, hear the sounds, taste the foods!

Behave as if.

TRY A NEW EXERCISE CLASS

I give two hours for this in case you need to drive to the class.

If you are opting for an online class, you can take your time getting into workout clothes and take a shower afterward if you feel like it.

This one is similar to trying a new workout, but instead of doing it on your own you are attending a class. I mean, you are registering for and joining a scheduled class. You never know, you might make a new friend.

You will be surprised how strong and brave you will feel after finishing this one, even if you are not any good at the actual workout. The goal is to have fun trying a new thing with other people.

GRATITUDE BOARD

A gratitude board looks a lot like a vision board. I heard the term "gratitude board" somewhere and grabbed on to it. The concept of a vision board is to create a visual tool that will help inspire you toward your goals. A gratitude board is similar, but it includes a few things you've already achieved. More on why that matters in a sec.

First, let me tell you, I was a poo-pooer of vision/ gratitude boards for the longest time because I did not understand how they worked. Sticking magazine pictures on poster board did nothing for me.

Yawn.

That is, until I understood how to connect vision boarding to actual emotion. Remember the visual cortex, the movie screen in your brain that cannot tell the difference between real and imagined? We are tapping into that again. That is the picture part of the board.

As you create your board, get in touch with your emotions. When you imagine yourself having whatever it is you are putting on the board, how does it feel? When you see the picture and feel that emotion, it is powerful! Remember "behave as if"? See yourself achieving the goal that is on the board.

When you see images of things you already imagined happening, your brain thinks, "Oh, we can have all these things," and once your brain is on board... things start to fall into place.

Combine emotion and the visual cortex... *magic*!!!!!

As for how to make a vision board? *So* many options!

I would say find some old magazines rather than buying new, because they are wildly more expensive than I remember them being back when I had a subscription to *Seventeen*. Check with neighbors, doctor's/ dentist's offices, and even thrift stores. You can also get pictures from the internet – I like this because when I do it, I find even more things to shoot for. I'm a basic board creator. I print some pictures from the internet and glue them to poster board. I like a collage look: images somewhat overlapping, organizing the images wherever they feel good to me at the time. I've seen very organized boards as well. I have one client who uses a corkboard and pins her pictures on it because she likes being able to update it easily. You can also create a digital vision board.

So how you make it is totally up to you. My only rule is: *have fun!*

To give your board a turbo-boost, you can add the words "Thank You" and include images that represent goals you have already achieved. It is a brain hack.

Put the board where you will see it regularly, but make sure you intentionally notice it and it does not become visual noise that you ignore. I have a client who lovingly touches each image and says "thank you" each day.

Mine is up in my office, in my direct line of sight when I sit at my desk. I make sure to notice each image and say "thank you" every day. I also have a picture of my board as the screensaver on my phone.

The best part of vision boarding is that you can do it however you want. Get creative and, again, have fun!

SELF-CARE BOARD OR JAR

I will admit, I am a bit of a hoarder when it comes to self-care ideas. There is no possible way for me to incorporate every self-care tool I know into my life at one time.

For a while, I would keep a notebook for writing all the ideas down. But it is not like I carry that with me and review it regularly, so I came up with the board idea.

I use poster board for this, and it looks a bit like a ransom note because I cut a lot of the ideas out of magazines or from articles I print. Some is handwritten. It is not pretty. It is not ugly. It is utilitarian. Both sides are covered and I hang it on my wall with one of those black and silver paper clip thingies (I had to Google what those are called – binder clips!) so I can flip it over when I get bored with one side. When I am in the mood for something different in my self-care game, I look at the board and something always pops out for me.

The jar serves a similar purpose, except it is even more

random. I write different self-care ideas on small pieces of paper, fold them up, and toss them in the jar. Needing inspiration for how to take care of yourself? Just reach in and grab one.

You could even use the ideas in this book for your jar or board! Easy peasy.

TAKE THE CLASS

My newsfeeds are always full of course offerings, probably because I am frequently looking to learn new things. This lets me know that there is no shortage of opportunity if you want to learn something new.

What do you wish you knew how to do? What is interesting to you? What would make your life easier if you knew how to do it? What seems like fun?

There is a class for everything. I am sure of it. I mean, I have not actually verified that, but I'll bet that if you want to learn it, there is a class for it.

If you have not been eyeballing a class already, check out the websites Udemy and Teachable. You will get some ideas for sure. Your local Community Education catalog/ website is also a good source.

You get to learn whatever you want to learn. Go for it!

THREE HOURS

SPLURGE ON NEW/ ALTERNATIVE TREATMENTS

*T*his can be amazingly wonderful, or it can be, well, um… not.

I was given a gift certificate for a hydro-massage for my birthday a couple years ago. I practice what I preach, so I went for it. I like a good massage, and I am a Pisces. Seemed like a perfect match!

It was not my favorite. I gained tension during the massage and, if I am really honest, I have to say "massage" is a misnomer. But I am glad I tried it. It makes me laugh when I think of how uncomfortable I was.

Please do not let me dissuade you – it could be exactly right for you!

Anyway – most of us are pretty good about our doctor and dentist appointments. Some of us may even include chiropractor and massage appointments regularly.

Trying something new or alternative is a good way to add more options to your indulgence list.

Have you ever done float therapy? I *love* it. I did not try it for quite a while because, for some reason, I thought you had to float naked in a pitch-black pod and that made me feel like puking. In actuality, you can choose your lighting and it is more like a giant bathtub, totally private and secure. I think I fall asleep, but I'm not sure.

This list is not all-inclusive, but it will give you some ideas for new treatments to try:

- Massage
- Sauna
- Chiropractor
- Acupuncture
- Acupressure
- Emotional Freedom Technique/ tapping
- Craniosacral therapy
- Reiki
- Chakra work

While you can do some of these for yourself, it's always nice to work with a professional. Think of it like this: you can make a sandwich for yourself, but don't they just taste better at a restaurant? And the professionals are most likely better at their craft than you are.

How will you know if you like it if you never try it?

TRY SOMETHING NEW

Anything.

I went to one of those indoor skydiving places last year. I definitely had to B.S it 'til I finessed it, as my sixteen-year-old says. I had to stand around longer than I wanted to, dressed in a flight suit that felt too small, but once I was in the air... it was worth it. I totally wish it had lasted longer!

You don't have to skydive, but pick something you have never done… and do it.

Groupon is a cool way to get ideas and a deal on something you may never do again. Take a look at the "Things To Do" category.

Remember, if you're not having fun, you're doing it wrong!

GRIT LIST

Three hours may be too long for this one, but you want to make sure you have time to do it properly! I heard this idea on a podcast.

We all have those things we put off and put off and put off. I once snoozed a reminder to make my dentist appointment for eight months. One. Week. At. A. Time.

Seriously? Yes.

When I moved, it took me three months to get my address changed in all the places I needed to change it. I am honestly not sure I got them all, because I never made a list.

The Grit List is a way to crank it out and be done. It is super simple.

Step 1: Make a list of all the phone calls, emails, and online changes you need to make.

Step 2: Sit down and get them done.

You can do this weekly, monthly, quarterly, annually, once in your life… you choose how often and how long you want that list to be. The feeling you get when it is done is *so* worth the doing.

COOK A BEAUTIFUL MEAL

I give this one three hours in case you want to clean up.

Whether you have a favorite recipe or want to try a new one, the idea here is that you completely enjoy the process.

Listen to the sounds: the chopping, the water boiling, the sizzle.

Look at all the colors. So many different colors created by nature. Create a beautiful presentation.

Feel the textures as you prepare your meal. The weight of the knife. The heat of the stove.

Smell the aromas. See if you can pick different things out by smell.

Taste… *ahhh*… taste your results. Sit and enjoy your meal. Take your time. Put your fork down between bites. Savor your food.

And, if you want, leave the dishes.

WRITE A VISION STORY

Yours, specifically. This is a very powerful exercise when done fully. When I say "fully," I mean with total connection to the story on your part.

The idea is, of course, that you write a story. It can be just one page, or many. You write it as if you have already achieved something you really want. You can write it like a newspaper story. Or you can just write it freeform, no rules. The story is about you, how you feel, and how your life is amazing because you have achieved whatever it is you wanted to achieve.

It could be one thing or a bunch of things that have made your life better. You are the author!

Say you want to lose fifteen pounds. Write a story about walking into a room of people, wearing a spectacular outfit in the size you want to be! How does it feel? How does it change your life? What emotions do you tap into?

Maybe you want to leave a corporate job and start your own business. Write a story about a week in the life of you – business owner! What is that like? What do you do when you are in charge of your own schedule? What does the future look like now that you are the boss?

See how it works? The story needs to include a lot of emotion and description. When you read it, you should feel a bit cringey for being so bold. That means you are onto something. Then read it to yourself on the regular. The more you read it, the more it seems like you can make it reality!

PICNIC

So simple!

Fill a basket or cooler with your favorite foods and beverages, grab a blanket, find a nice place to sit, and enjoy!

You do not have to go far – you can do this in the backyard if you want. Or you can take a little road trip to a park or other outdoor spot. Wherever you end up, relish the food and take in the world around you.

You could read a book or take a snooze if the mood is there.

You will feel like you got away from it all afterward – and who doesn't want that every now and then?

MASSAGE

I know that massage shows up more than once in this book. I am a fan!

This one is in the three-hour category to allow for transit time… *and* an extra five to ten minutes for you to just lie still immediately after the massage and let the bodywork soak in.

Many options are available for massage: hot stones, essential oils… some even offer infrared light treatments. Add the extra foot massage or facial.

This is your chance to truly pamper yourself. Get the extras.

FULL HAIR AND MAKEUP

I could have completely miscategorized this one, because I never dry my hair. If I did it would be full, that's for sure. Until I got nervy enough to stand up to hair stylists and leave salons with my hair wet, I would look in the mirror at what they'd done to my head and wonder if the stylists and I were looking at the same thing.

I digress.

If this does not take you three hours, add some other ideas to the schedule.

The idea is to glam yourself up to your ideal level of glam.

Maybe you deep-condition your hair and do a face masque and spend the day enjoying your natural beauty. Could be you go all the way to full contouring and false lashes. Everyone's level is different. You do you.

This one is good (especially during a quarantine) when you realize it's been two days since you showered, and you are not sure you can pull off a messy bun again.

… At least, so I've heard…

You could also put on real clothes if you're feeling bold. Pay attention to how you feel – it changes.

WINDOW SHOP AND BUY THE OUTFIT

This is about leisure.

It is not about trying on a bunch of clothes and getting

frustrated.

Take your time and mosey (walk sort of aimlessly but with some purpose – I made that definition up!) through your favorite local retail spot. Maybe it's a mall. Maybe it's a boutique. Who knows? Not me.

When you see pieces that make you smile, choose them. Put together an outfit. Shoes too!

It does not have to be fancy – it can be casual! Do you like jewelry? Get some. Want a purse? Add that.

Not ready to purchase? Take pictures and add them to your gratitude board! But enjoy the experience.

———

✎ You got it – book the time! Find a spot on your calendar for a three-hour session of self-care. (I almost wrote "a three-hour tour" but I'm not sure how many *Gilligan's Island* fans are reading this. If you are – ahoy and sorry you have the theme song stuck in your head now.)

———

14

HALF-DAY

SOLO MINI-ROAD TRIP

I did this much more frequently before I had kids. There are really no rules to this one! You get in your car and drive. You can plan it ahead, or not.

I would often pick a direction and drive until I got somewhere I wanted to stop.

That somewhere may have been a roadside flea market, a café, or a cute row of shops in a small town. It might have been a gas station because I had to pee and there was nothing else on the trip.

I would give myself a time or mile limit and, when I hit that, I had to turn around and head home.

Sometimes, I would have a specific destination in mind.

The purpose was not to get somewhere, though. It was to enjoy the drive.

Think about what is just beyond where you live. What is just beyond that?

Go find out!

VOLUNTEER

It feels good to give.

Growing up, I did not know much about volunteerism. I guess this was because, as a single working mom, my mother did not have time or energy, but I'm not really sure.

I first learned about volunteering when I started my corporate job (my bank teller job a gazillion years ago) and each employee was given eight hours per year (paid!) to volunteer. I was all over that! I think it increased to sixteen hours over the time I was there, but I don't know for sure because, after a couple years, I didn't care if I got paid.

It is pretty easy to find ways to do this. Google is a great place to start! The NextDoor app is also handy for this. Your local school or church can definitely use help... animal shelters, too!

There is no shortage of need for people who want to help. We all have something to offer.

DONATE

Dovetailing off the volunteer idea, donation follows pretty naturally. While actual donating does not take a half-day, you can take the time to prepare your donations. (Unless they're money. Then it will just take a minute!)

Volunteering is simply donating your time and/ or skills. Donating old clothes and household items is common and needed.

Some other ways I have found to donate are:

- Keep kits in my car for when I see people on corners with signs. These kits contain things like snacks, hygiene items, socks, and one-dollar and five-dollar bills.

- Take feminine hygiene items to a women's shelter (diapers, etc. as well).
- Keep restaurant/grocery store gift-cards handy for when people ask for money/ food.
- Pay it forward: when you're in line, offer to pay for someone else in line.

AT-HOME SPA EXPERIENCE

Using the ideas in earlier sections as a spa menu, create your perfect experience at home.

Maybe that looks like an Epsom salt bath with essential oils followed by some yummy skincare and a mani/ pedi. Or you can add your own luxurious treatments.

Whatever makes you feel pampered, do that.

Plan it, make any preparations necessary (including asking for help if you have kids), and lose yourself in your own pampering.

Remember to engage all the senses. Candles, music, snacks… make it wonderful.

SHOP FOR AND PREPARE A MEAL ENTIRELY FROM THE FARMER'S MARKET

If a farmer's market isn't available to you, check out the organic section of your local grocery store. Try to find a small store rather than a large chain if you want more of the farm-to-table feel. You might even be able to find a local farm that sells to the public. It does not get more farm-to-table than that!

Wherever you go for your ingredients, enjoy your time there. You could either have a list of exactly what you need to make your meal or be a wild adventurer and buy whatever grabs your attention and see how it comes together.

When you get home, take your time preparing the meal. Enjoy the process: the sound of chopping vegetables... the aromas mixing... the sizzle and bubble. See how beautiful you can make your meal.

Eat it in a beautiful spot and enjoy each bite to its fullest.

You can even leave the dishes for later. They will still be there.

TAKE YOURSELF ON A DATE

What is your idea of a perfect date? Why wait for someone to take you on it?

You can plan the date yourself and enjoy your own company.

Get ready the way you would for someone else, with all the pampering you want. Take a bubble bath. Condition your hair. Shave your legs. Put your favorite outfit on – even if it's jeans and a sweatshirt.

When you are confident enough to go on out on your own, you create all sorts of new options for yourself.

BINGE WATCH

Snuggle in and watch your favorite series/ movies for hours.

Dim the lights and enjoy a scented candle.

Remember to include snacks and beverages.

If you fall asleep, no worries, because a nap is totally self-care, too!

PURGE YOUR WARDROBE

I love this one when the mood hits me. I am usually pretty perplexed about how I end up with so many clothes between wardrobe purges. I am not a shopper! (Come to think of it, I have not really had to do this much since I left my corporate job. Especially not this year! Living in pajamas and joggers is kind of my jam during a pandemic, I suppose.)

This works the same way as when you sorted your drawers. Take *every*thing out and make a giant pile somewhere. I usually end up not being able to see much of my bed.

Have your bins or bags ready, again divided into donate, store, and trash. If you can tell where an item is going to end up when you grab it, you do not even have to put it in the main pile. Touch it once if possible.

Get serious about whether you really need or want each item.

I kept a cocktail dress (tags still on it) in my closet for years. Anyone who knows me would probably be laughing out loud to hear that! The dress was pretty. I got a good deal on it. It had no sentimental value. I finally donated it when I realized that, should the fancy event opportunity ever arise, I might have different tastes, be in a different mood, or be an entirely different size.

Puh-leeze! Clear the way for stuff you love and will use! Do not keep things just in case. If you have not worn something in a year, do you really love it?

Once everything is sorted, put your keepers back in your closet/ drawers and put the donate items right in your car so you can drive around with them in your car for a year before you finally get to Goodwill or wherever you are taking them.

I jest... I cannot imagine doing that.

...Or can I?

MUSEUM/ KID'S MUSEUM

Sometimes I don't really understand what I'm looking at in museums. And that's okay! The fun is just taking the time to peruse at your own pace.

I once volunteered to chaperone my daughter's fourth-grade class at a fancy (and huge) art museum. Note – this is not self-care, but it is a hilarious story. Apparently, museums only invite elementary kids *all on the same day*! It felt like there were a trillion children. It was so crowded! My only job was to make sure I got back to the entrance with my twelve kids. As the day wore on, I noticed a similar expression on all the chaperones' faces – a mix of panic and weariness – as we continually counted our children over and over again to make sure we had not lost any.

It was just about time to make our way to the entrance. As I scoped out my escape, I saw two different paths, one longer than the other. But taking the short one would mean we would be passing through an exhibit that, at a glance, appeared to be all naked people. It was very Renaissance-y.

I went for the short one, thinking I would just ignore any silly kids' jokes and we'd get through. I will note, I was the only chaperone who took this path. The kids could not resist circling around the life-sized statue with the penis right at their eye-level... so many giggles. We were almost through the section when, right in front of us, was a massive painting of a nude woman lounging on a fancy couch, apparently in the forest. She had the back of her hand against her forehead and her eyes were closed.

One little girl piped up and said, "She must have had a *really* hard day at work!"

I was laughing so hard on the inside. I agreed with her and we made our way to the entrance to load the bus that was waiting for us.

All humor aside, you can really enjoy yourself at a museum. Take your time at each exhibit. Really notice the objects or pieces of art. Think about the artist and imagine what their life was like when they created the object/ art. If you love something, why? If something is not interesting to you, why not? Stop and have a snack or lunch if it is available to you.

Leisurely is your goal.

———

Spend a few moments thinking about these activities. Which is the most attractive to you? Imagine an entire half-day for you. Go schedule it.

———

15

WHOLE DAYS AND FULL WEEKENDS

TOUR YOUR TOWN

*H*ave you enjoyed all your town/ city has to offer? If you are a local, chances are the answer is no.

Do it. Pretend you are a tourist visiting from another state or even country. Get some pamphlets. (Wait, is it 1990? Sometimes I forget.)

Go online and look up your locale. They almost all have tourist information! Plan a day to get to know your city.

If you do already know your hometown well, pick another location that is close enough to drive to and explore there.

Look around with new eyes and see what you find!

DIAL IT BACK

I first started this when I worked in corporate, but it works everywhere.

Any time you are amped up or agitated about something, it is likely you have invested more than your fair share of energy into it. And sometimes… *sometimes*, that is necessary.

Usually it's not. Let's talk about work first.

Going along with the productivity myth, we start by giving 100%. Then, when something requires more, we increase to 110%… 120%… and so on. It is not sustainable, and you can feel it.

Take a moment and decide how much effort you need to put into doing your job well. It probably isn't 100% *all the time*. I know it's not. So pick the percentage to aim for for most of your work. Let's say it's 80%.

You will figure out what 80% is by paying attention to your feelings throughout your day. If everything is going smoothly, right on. If you are struggling to get something done, you may need to up it to 85 or 90% temporarily. Any time you get pissed about something, you need to dial it down.

I was giving a solid 50% of my energy to my job at the end of my corporate career, and the vast majority of that was going to my team and not directly to the company. When I joined two other leaders to interview candidates to replace me, I upped it to 100%. When leadership chose the candidate we (unanimously) listed as the lowest qualified and least suited for the position, I dialed it down to about 20%.

At no time did the business suffer based on my energy level. I knew what needed to get done and it always got done. To be clear, I am not advising you to slack off; I am saying you should know what percentage of your energy is needed to do the job and not go above that level unless you want to.

When I wanted a promotion or a raise, up went the energy I put into the job.

Think of your energy like a spectrum and adjust accordingly.

Be intentional. The system would have you at 100% (or

more!) all the time. That is not necessary. Know when good enough is good enough.

Along those lines, let's talk about relationships. Though our motivation to overperform in relationships is different than what it is at work, the energy spectrum still applies.

To simplify this concept (since it probably deserves its own book), if you are giving more to the relationship than the other person is, dial it back. If you are afraid to do that because you think the relationship will suffer, know that the relationship is already suffering because *you* are suffering.

Give it a try though. We teach people how to treat us. Just because they are used to you giving more doesn't mean they can't learn a new way to relate to you.

Communication is important here. If you are going to change things up, it is possible that you need to mention it. For example, if laundry is where you are going to conserve your energy, ask someone else to do it (or deal with huge piles later). When you commit to taking time for self-care, ask for help or time or support.

Dial it back and see how it goes. You may be pleasantly surprised.

Once you are comfortable dialing it back for a day, move it into your ongoing routine.

SPA DAY

Book yourself a full day of pampering. That is all.

A DAY OF ONLY POSITIVE SELF-TALK

This one needs to be ongoing, but we will start with one day, then add it into your rotation regularly.

We can be so unkind to ourselves. If you paid attention to the things you say to yourself – often in your head – and imagined saying them out loud to someone you love, you would be appalled.

We have around six thousand thoughts per day. Our thoughts create our reality. What kind of reality are you creating if you talk shit about yourself? I know what kind – I have lived it.

But no more! About six years ago I started conditioning my brain for positive self-talk. Here's how: I made myself say the exact opposite of my shit-talk. For example, one of my go-to thoughts was "I do not deserve that anyway. How stupid of me." I'd think this about whatever it was I wanted – usually, somebody treating me a certain way.

So what I would say when I noticed that thought was, "I deserve that and *more*! I will accept nothing less!" I would say it out loud. At first, it felt ridiculous and bogus. But I kept going. Eventually, the nasty thoughts came less and less often until, when I had one, *it* would sound ridiculous and bogus.

We are all different, every single one of us. For some of you, silly and *super* exaggerated is the way to go. For others, just speaking rationally will do the trick. Maybe simply speaking facts will do it.

Here is a beautiful example of the different ways this can be done. (I am shamelessly stealing from a peer here):

- Negative thought: "My nose is huge and so ugly!"
- Over-exaggeration: "I have the most incredible nose on earth! People bow to the beauty of my perfect schnoz!"
- Opposite but rational and true: "My nose is a great size for my face and makes me look like my mom. It's cool to be able to see someone I love when I look in the mirror."
- Just the facts, ma'am: "My nose lets me smell beautiful things. Even if I don't like how it looks, I'm

> grateful that I can smell my favorite things: cookies
> in the oven, freshly mowed grass, flowers, etc."

Today, I cannot remember the last time I had a negative thought about myself. And you know what? I expect no less from others with whom I have relationships. See how that works?

WEAR SEXY UNDERWEAR

I do not know what this means to you. We all have our favorite style of undies. It could be a thong, or maybe it's boxer briefs.

The point of this one is to wear something under your clothes that helps you feel sexy. It doesn't mean anyone else will even see it!

Have a sexy bra and panty set? Put it on under your sweats. Love that boyshort and tank set? Do it!

If you normally grab your underwear out of the drawer without looking and rotate between your two comfy bras hanging on the back of your closet door, adding this as a regular option is going to make you feel differently no matter what you wear.

THANK YOU FOR UNDERSTANDING

Say this instead of "sorry." All. Day. Long. Yep. You read that right.

(Okay, not when you need to give an apology because you have hurt someone or caused damage to something. In those situations, "I am sorry" is appropriate.)

"Thank you for understanding" is for all the other times "sorry" pops out of your mouth without you even thinking.

We are so ready to apologize for taking up space and being human.

Like when you are a running a few minutes behind to meet a friend: "Thanks for understanding that I may have overscheduled myself today."

Or if you make a mistake: "Thanks for understanding. I will try again/ do better next time."

"Thanks for understanding" allows the other person to know you need some grace.

Don't we all?

NO, THANK YOU

Remember the very beginning of this book? Well, here we are working that "no" muscle!

Spend one whole day saying "no, thank you" when you do not want to do or have something.

That's it. Simple! Do not say "yes" when you want to say "no."

Notice how it's okay. Notice how you enjoy your day more.

WATCH YOUR LANGUAGE AND ASK BETTER QUESTIONS

You are probably noticing a theme here. Remember way back in the five-minute section when I wrote about giving meaning with words? Well, that's the deal here, too. We are just leveling up to a whole day so you can build a new pattern.

Pay attention to your words. What do you say often that makes things more difficult? Here are some examples of words or phrases to notice: "why me," "hard," "challenging," "difficult," "impossible," "bad," "wrong," "cannot," "hate," and "never."

That list is certainly not conclusive, but you get the gist. When you notice one of these words in your mind or coming out of your mouth, say something different instead. If you play with this, it is more fun and you will change your habit quicker.

Here are some ideas:

- "Why is it so easy?"
- "Why is this the best thing to happen to me?"
- "Why do I love doing this?"
- "What will I learn from this?"

These are all great examples of questions to ask yourself to break your pattern of disservice through language. Something will come to you.

MENTAL HEALTH DAY

I believe it is important that we all prioritize ourselves enough that we can just say, "I am taking a day off because I need one."

I want my daughters to believe that before they are middle-aged, so I taught them about mental health days a couple of years ago. They will ask me to excuse them from school for a mental health day a couple times of a year now – and I do it without question. I would even do it if they asked more frequently. Their moods improve, their focus is better, and they know they deserve to take care of themselves.

For you, my friend, I recommend taking a day when you feel like you just can't deal with your life or the world or your partner or your kids or the cat. Take the day. Do whatever feels good.

Even better is if you are proactive about it and schedule these before it is a "Calgon, take me away" situation. (If you have no idea what I'm talking about, you're young and you can Google it. I just did and there was one search result that had the phrase "vintage '70s commercial" in it. I am vintage. I love it!)

You would not expect your vehicle to continue to turn on if you did not fill it with gas, would you?

Fill your tank. This is a chance to take a whole day and schedule it with self-care.

DECLUTTER YOUR HOME

The first time I did this, I was amazed by how much more space I had when I was finished. I am fairly good at keeping a tidy house, but over time, well, stuff happens.

I had my standard bins – donate, toss, and storage. I moved from room to room using Marie Kondo's method of asking, "Does this spark joy?" about each item. Again, very simply, if an item does not spark joy, it goes in a bin (I go over this in more detail in "Declutter Your Space" in Chapter 11). You can watch Marie Kondo in action on Netflix.

In my situation, almost everything went in a bin. Most of the storage items were things I had received as gifts from my kids or relatives.

You could also include a "sell" bin, if you're into that. I recently sold several pieces of furniture on Facebook Marketplace and that was pretty simple. But if it involves me taking something somewhere else to sell it, I am probably not up for that. Know thyself!

Funny story about those storage bins. I recently moved and I barely have any storage space. Even in the garage, there is only enough room for about a third of the bins we moved in with. This meant that I got to declutter my bins! As I was going through them and found bins full of stuff I had gone through during previous decluttering sessions, I wondered why I had not just donated some of them originally. Sometimes I play a good game of kick-the-can-down-the-road with myself!

Also, as an aside, if you are saving all the papers your kids brought home from elementary school with the idea they'll want to take them when they move out, you can probably check in with your kids and get rid of those bins.

…Oh, is that just me?

DEEP CLEAN YOUR HOME

A long long time ago in a galaxy far far away, I cleaned my home top-to-bottom every Saturday. I had a ritual after I cleaned: I lit a scented candle and ate a bagel with jelly while I listened to my favorite CD, probably Cher.

Granted, at the time my home was a one-bedroom duplex, and you could stand in the middle and see all four rooms: kitchen, bathroom, living room, and bedroom. It was so cute.

I continued that habit – cleaning everything once a week – way longer than I should have. It is one thing to manage the tiny duplex and another when it is a four-bedroom, two-to-three story situation. Somewhere along the line, I created the story that if it all was not clean *at the same time*, it was never really clean. I would get so stressed out trying to find time to make it happen!

Eventually, I realized it was okay to get to it in sections. That is how I handle it now. Everything gets deep-cleaned about once a month – I have a rotation!

Also, I figured out that I did not need to have my home ready for guests who might drop by unannounced like I was a housewife in the fifties. That's not how I roll anyway, not to mention that I don't think it's ever happened once in my entire life. If someone is really my friend and drops by, they will understand if my house isn't ready for a HGTV filming!

However, there is something nice about getting everything shiny and clean (all at the same time) every now and then.

So that is how I do it. When the mood strikes – *every now and then*.

Give it a try. It feels really good to sit and admire your work, even if it only lasts for a moment.

DAY OF GRATITUDE

This is a day when you allow yourself to focus on all the reasons you are grateful. It really helps to set the intention and say "thank you" out loud as you notice your gratitude.

Another great idea is to tell people in your life why you are grateful for them. You can send a text or make a call. Leave a note if they're in your home.

Maybe spend some time writing about all the things you have gratitude for, or consider a guided meditation about gratitude.

If you have ever read *The Magic* by Rhonda Byrne, open it to a random page and use that as your main focus throughout the day. If you have not read it, you may want to consider making that purchase.

Spend the day spreading gratitude all around, and you will fall asleep with a smile on your face.

SOCIAL MEDIA DETOX

Simple but maybe not easy, this will leave you feeling like you have way more time to spend on things that make a difference in your life.

Delete the apps from your phone for a full day and do not sign on anywhere else.

FULL WEEKEND

Solo Mini Vacation

By the time you are up to a full weekend of self-care, you do not need much instruction!

A fun way to incorporate this is to have a wish-list. Start a journal where you write down the places you want to go or the things you will enjoy when you enough time. This can be an actual traveling experience, or you can stay at home. The rule is that you must enjoy yourself.

Remember, when your tank is full, you're better at everything you do. Taking a weekend to yourself will benefit everyone you are special to. Your kids, partner, lover, family, friends… they'll all get the better version of you when you love yourself enough to spend a weekend enjoying yourself.

Everything will be okay – even if you're out of pocket for two days.

Whatever your heart desires, plan it, then do it.

Mini Vacation – Girls' Trip

See above. Invite a friend or two (or five).

–––––––

✎ Before you tell me I've lost my mind…pick one of these. Put it on your calendar. With a smiley-face by it.

–––––––

16

ONGOING SELF-CARE

*T*his chapter could just be two words: do it.

The whole point of this book is to get to a mindset that means taking care of yourself is the only option.

Any self-care can be ongoing if you do it consistently. I am sharing the ones I find most commonly used on an ongoing basis. This does not mean you have to do all of these every day. Many of these ideas have been covered in more detail earlier in the book. Some are pretty self-explanatory.

You will notice I spend more words on the bedtime and morning routines than the other ideas in the book. That is because you get the most bang for your buck if you incorporate some version of these routines into your life.

The key to ongoing self-care is to schedule it. Some of these are daily ideas, some less frequently included.

Schedule your self-care. Whatever you do for the rest of the things you schedule, do the same thing for self-care. Phone calendar? Do it. Family calendar on the fridge? Do it. Planner you carry everywhere? Do it. This time is every bit as important as carpool plans and work meetings.

BEDTIME ROUTINE

OOOOoooooooohhhhh. Do this one first! Trust me.

Your morning routine actually starts with your bedtime routine.

A bedtime routine can be as short or long as you want it to be, but to really relax into bed, go for thirty minutes at a minimum. And if you want a solid morning routine, it starts here.

First, some math is needed. Think about how much sleep you optimally need. Then, based on your ideal wake-up time, back the clock up to determine when you should be asleep – in dreamland, not just getting into bed. Estimate how long it typically takes you to fall asleep (this should change over time as you implement a solid bedtime routine). Once you have that, back into the start time of your bedtime routine.

Here's an example:

I prefer eight hours of sleep and want to wake up at 6:15 a.m.

To get eight hours of sleep and wake up at 6:15, I need to be sleeping by 10:15 p.m. With my bedtime routine, it takes me about fifteen minutes to fall asleep, so I need to be in bed, lights off, no later than 10:00 p.m.

To manage this for a thirty-minute bedtime routine, I'll set an alarm for 9:00 p.m. Then I'll finish whatever I'm doing and start my bedtime routine by 9:30 p.m. at the latest.

Phone alarms are your friend while you are establishing a routine. Do not hesitate to use them.

Here is what I do every night: journal, quick review of the next day's schedule, light a scented candle, brush my teeth, get my pj's on, and do my skincare.

I like a little variety – and if I am honest, I need it, or I get bored and stop doing the routine – so I have a list of things I *can* do but don't do them all every night. Think of it like a salad bar or buffet: all the food choices are there, but you don't eat them all every time.

Here is what I rotate in and out of my routine:

- Yin yoga
- Qi gong
- Tai chi
- Meditation
- Reading
- Foam rolling
- Stretching
- Tapping
- Bath

You create what is perfect for you and adjust as needed. Be flexible.

MORNING ROUTINE

This is a great way to set the tone for your day. Before I figured this out, I lurched out of bed, showered with my eyes half-open, got dressed, poured some coffee to drink cold later (when I remembered I had even poured it), got the kids ready and off to school, and started my work day.

Familiar?

The math is easier for this routine. Figure out when you need to officially start your day – whatever that is for you – and wake up early enough to complete your routine. This will be a work in progress until you find your rhythm. Give yourself some grace.

My morning routine varies in length. Some days it is thirty to sixty minutes, and some days it is ninety minutes to two hours (weekends). I use the same method I wrote about for my bedtime routine.

Here are my "always do"s: brush teeth, make my tea, make breakfast for the kids, do some kind of movement, listen to a podcast, do my skincare, put on mascara (I have the most invisible blonde eyelashes), journal, and meditate.

Here are my "rotate in and out" options:

- Shower*
- Yoga
- Foam roller
- Read
- Any one of my *many* workout programs purchased over the years
- Angel card reading
- Shave my legs
- Something else

I say this is a rotator because some days I just feel like a quick bits wash and messy bun – and that's perfectly okay!

The last thing I do is get dressed and head into my office.

My kids are old enough to fend for themselves, so they do not interfere at all, but if you have younger kids, note that it's okay for them to watch a show or two while you take care of yourself. It is also okay for them to understand how important it is to show yourself some care and love. They will think that is normal if they see you do it. *Mom win!!*

I cannot stress enough the importance of giving yourself grace and being flexible about these routines. The idea is not to do everything all the time, it is to give yourself what you need to feel the best you can feel.

Here is a story that I hope will help you to allow yourself to be human. Before I learned about the flexibility aspect of routines – or just made that up to suit my own needs – I had the idea that my routine had to be completely non-negotiable. I started various routines so many times and felt like a failure on many occasions. What kind of coach cannot complete a morning routine?

Here's what happened right before my flexibility epiphany.

I had dutifully completed every part of my routine except my morning meditation. I went into my bedroom and closed the door to hopefully not hear the morning chaos that was my children at the time. I laid down, turned on my guided meditation, and started my breathwork. Just as I started to relax into the meditation, some creature was bumping at my door – cat, dog, child, no idea. *Meditating harder. Ignoring my children's voices harder.* Starting to stress, knowing I would not be able to get in the zone in time to feel like I meditated. *Should I start over?* The bumping at the door got more aggressive. I was ignoring and meditating so hard! Then the perimeter was breached. It was the year-old black lab puppy. *Still meditating.* Fifty-pound puppy now lying on top of me... kids louder... dishes clanking... dog breathing in my face... tail wagging so hard... one earbud falling out.

I was *still* trying to meditate. My whole body was tensed up... my face crunched... eyes squeezed shut so hard... tears sliding down my cheeks into my ears... dog licking said tears. I was going to complete the damn routine because *I was not a failure*.

Friends, do not be like me that day. Give yourself grace and flexibility. It is *so* much better.

SCHEDULE HONESTLY

Our brains can be fickle organs. We can be so determined to focus on a specific task for a certain amount of time... and then check that *one* email or just check social media *really quickly*... and before we know it, an hour – or three – has passed.

What happened there is we overestimated how long our brain would let us focus on whatever we were attempting to focus on for too long.

The amount of time we can focus varies on what, when, and why we are focused. It changes.

The trick is to get ahead of the distraction train. Take a look at the tasks you have on your plate and get really honest about how long you can focus on each one.

Then schedule a break five minutes before that time is up. When I say "break," I do not mean laundry. I mean get up and have a one-song dance party or sit outside in the sun. A *real* break.

Haha! You beat your brain that way. If you are not sure how long you need between breaks, pay attention to when you start getting distracted. Right before that starts… that is how long you can focus.

We can certainly up our focus by connecting to an emotional purpose, but that is another book or podcast.

If you look at your calendar and see that you can block off four hours for a project you need to make a lot of progress on, awesome. Block the whole four hours, but do it in chunks. Schedule breaks.

It is important to get real with yourself.

I will share that twenty-five minutes of solid focus is not a bad thing.

Work for twenty-five minutes, listen to music and lip sync for five minutes, work for another twenty-five minutes, have a five-minute dance party, work for twenty-five minutes… and so on.

Have a lot of Zoom meetings? Dance your way to the bathroom between meetings. Or go off camera and do some pushups. One minute of break is sometimes good enough to get you back into the zone.

When you schedule honestly, you will be more productive when you need to produce.

SKINCARE ROUTINE

Ahhhh… your largest organ. Take care of it. Regularly.

There is a whole section on this earlier in the book so I will not spend more time on it here other than to say show yourself some love. You are beautiful and you deserve it.

GRATITUDE PRACTICE

I love gratitude. It feels so good!

The most important aspect of a gratitude practice is that you really connect emotionally to it.

Again, the book *The Magic* by Rhonda Byrne is fantastic at really defining a beautiful gratitude practice. I recommend it.

SLEEP IN

Maybe you are a morning person who easily wakes up with the sun (or before), full of energy. I am definitely impressed.

Maybe you are more like me and every now and then it feels really good to sleep 'til you wake up naturally. Go for it. If you need to make arrangements for kids and/or pets, do it. If it's just you, give yourself permission.

Then let your body do its thing and wake up when you're rested. Note: doing this will likely throw off your morning routine, so make adjustments.

Sweet dreams.

MEDITATION

I do a lot of guided meditations myself, but I also notice other opportunities and take them.

A walk can be very meditative. So can cooking or doing dishes. Anything you let clear your mind will do.

Back when I thought I could not or was not able to meditate, I found a very cool explanation on YouTube. In the video, a Buddhist monk explains that meditation is simple: you just have to occupy your monkey mind.

Your monkey mind is always looking for something to do. If you do not intentionally give it something, it starts throwing its own poop. That is when your thoughts seem to overpower you. When I was learning, I told my monkey mind to count my breaths. In one, out one, in two, out two, in three, out three… and so on.

Regularly adding meditation to your days will make a positive difference.

EXERCISE YOUR "NO" MUSCLE

This is an excellent practice. Say "no" when you mean "no." That is all.

VISION/ GRATITUDE BOARD MAINTENANCE

Give your board some self-care.

As you reach goals and achieve what is on your board, keep it updated. If you use poster board, you can stick new pictures right on top of the past images. Or there's always the corkboard idea!

Remember to express your gratitude – both for what you have and what you *will* have.

GET READY FOR THE DAY

… even if you are not leaving the house.

This is a nice way to focus on yourself. As comfortable as it can be to lounge about in pajama bottoms, a sweatshirt, and a messy bun, give yourself some pampering. Shower, skincare, and some clothes are all it takes. You can do makeup and hair if you really want to up the energy.

I have worked from home for over ten years. A few years ago, I was out shopping with my girls and I looked at a pair of jeans. My daughter said, "That's not really your style."

Curious, I asked what my style was.

"I dunno… maybe pajamas?" In my defense, they were my *daytime* pajamas.

Now I get dressed every day… at least out of the pj's and into the leggings.

PURGE YOUR SOCIAL MEDIA

I am pretty serious about limiting social media. Most of the clients I work with are on social media diets while they work with me. Hopefully, that continues when we finish working together.

Social media is designed to keep you on it. Notice how you feel after a few minutes of scrolling.

If something makes you feel bad, unfollow/ unfriend. If you have something in your feed that makes you feel bad… get rid of it. You can always go back to it later.

Social media is not where relationships happen. Do not expect it to do that. If you are online friends with someone because you feel like you must be, stop it. If you need to stop seeing their stuff in your feed, unfollow them.

Put your healthy relationships back into the real world, make connections a different way, and if you want to stay on social media, use it for something else. See the next section, Intentional Consumption of Media, for more about this.

INTENTIONAL CONSUMPTION OF MEDIA

I am not perfect at this, and I am consistently working to be better to myself. Once you have purged your social media feed, the next step is to fill it with good stuff.

Do *not* use social media for news unless you are following a verifiable source. You can get the paper or read news online if you want to gather serious information.

Do use social media for yummy, nutritious mind food. Find groups and pages that make you feel up instead of down.

Are you finding content that makes you laugh? Content that causes you to relax? Maybe something that helps you grow? Anything that makes you feel better.

What that is will be different for everyone. The cool part is that once you find something you like, the suggestions will keep coming. You can also Google something you are interested in, or shop for it on Amazon. This works to help you find more things you like online, as creepy as that is.

Do the same for TV and reading. If something brings you down, there is probably a good chance you do not need to consume it.

Don't get me wrong, I'm not telling you to stick your fingers in your ears, close your eyes, and say "la la la" to ignore the world around you. I am active in my community and I know what is going on in our country and world, and I feel the pain when I learn about some of those things. I do not need it to be sensationalized or politicized. I decide what I can control and I engage in ways I think will make a positive difference.

Find the good and be part of it.

WHY IS IT SO EASY?

I love love *love* this one!

Any time I am struggling or stuck in a story that does not serve me, if I ask, "Why is it *sooooo* easy for me to [whatever I am struggling with]?" I feel better really quickly.

For instance, if my issue is that I am not motivated to work out, I will ask, "Why is it *sooooo* easy for me to start my morning workout?" over and over until it feels easy. Try it! Think of something you have procrastinated. Then ask yourself why it is so easy to get it done.

The first time you ask yourself this question will feel dumb. Keep going. If you ask the same question five to ten times in a row, by the last time you will feel way better about doing the task.

You do not even have to have a specific task in mind. I use this one when I cannot seem to figure out the solution to something. *Why is it* soooo *easy for me to solve this problem?*

Why is it so easy?

FEEL THE FEELINGS

Did you know that if you allow yourself to fully process an emotion it can be done in ninety seconds or less?

To do that, you need to simply feel the emotion. It will dissipate on its own.

We tend to do everything in our power not to feel bad or sad or frustrated or anything negative. We try to shake things off and move on. "Stiff upper lip" and all that.

Or alternatively, we really dig into an emotion and focus on all the ways we have been victimized.

In the first scenario, we create a toddler with a tantrum. That feeling is going to be felt, and the more we ignore it, the more it is on the ground kicking and screaming for attention.

By attempting to ignore a feeling, we make it worse. We also create a kind of scar in our energy flow... a blockage.

In the second scenario, the goal is to make it worse... to make ourselves the victim of the hugest wrong. We continue to focus on and think about how bad we feel. That is where resentments come in... we are re-sending a feeling to our brain repeatedly.

In either scenario, the emotional trauma can last for years... for a lifetime, even. And it sucks.

If you give yourself ninety seconds to be observant of what you are feeling, honor it... notice it... and then react with a nice balance of self-care, the emotion is processed. Do not give it any more meaning.

Because you have not been doing that your whole life, you have emotional scars. This means that sometimes, you just need to ugly cry in the bathroom with the door closed. Maybe you need to punch a pillow. Could be you need someone to hold you while you weep your eyes out. When you are ready, you can grow beyond the scars.

Do not be afraid of your feelings. Honor them. They are not too much. Never let anyone tell you that.

Think of yourself like the sky. Emotions are the weather. They will always pass if you let them.

———

✎ Pick one new ongoing self-care strategy to start with. Make a sticky note or phone alarm to remind you. Give yourself the grace to create a new pattern.

———

CREATE YOUR ENVIRONMENT

*W*hen you are in a place that feels supportive, you are going to be more likely to take care of yourself. So create your own sanctuary. Make your home (or at least your room) a place you genuinely enjoy. It is your sacred space. You deserve to feel good.

SCENTED CANDLES

This one is not for you if smells are not your jam. Obvi.

I lived most of my married life without scented candles and I don't know why. I love smells. I mean, good ones. Not like skunks or poop.

There was one episode – a brief separation – during which I bought scented candles. It made me so happy. I have had them going ever since. (Not the same candles. I get new ones.)

I have my favorites and I tend to have seasonal preferences. I just love love *love* the way they make me feel.

Pro-tip: make sure you smell your candles before you buy them – never go by scent name. I was in Target recently –

probably the second time this year – because I needed candles. Do you have any idea how hard it is to test scents through a mask? It is kind of impossible. I ended up with two good ones and a dud.

MUSIC

Music can soothe the soul or bump up your energy. It can do anything you want it to do if you pick the right song. Remember to use music. Even if you do not do lyrics, there is something about music that connects and changes your energy.

PHONE IN THE KITCHEN OVERNIGHT

There is not a lot to say about this. There are a ton of studies showing that the light from devices makes it difficult to fall asleep. So does scrolling social media and answering work emails (see the earlier section on intentional media consumption in Chapter 16).

Get an alarm clock.

SEPARATION OF WORK AND PERSONAL

While this has always been somewhat difficult, it got really sketchy in 2020 when we were all home most of the time.

It is so so so important to transition from work to home, even – no, *especially* – when you work at home.

If you are used to working somewhere else, the drive or commute can be a great transition between your work and personal life. Minus that, it's up to you to create the transition.

A few things to consider:

Do you get paid enough to be electronically available 24/ 7? The answer is probably no.

What is the longest amount of time someone will have to wait for your response if you do not touch your computer/ answer emails on your phone until the next morning? The answer is not exceptionally long.

Do you tell yourself that if you respond to work emails/ texts during personal time, you will not get behind at work? Is that really true? See the previous question.

Does anyone else's lack of planning constitute an emergency for you? The answer needs to be no.

Do you stay connected to work because you are afraid not to? Think about what that is doing to your mental state.

Now, stick with me here. Pick a time you can commit to closing your laptop/ ignoring your emails each day. Let's say it's 6:00 p.m. Set an alarm for 5:30 p.m. That is your warning bell. Figure out what you need to do to feel okay about closing up shop in the next thirty minutes. Set a second alarm for 6:00 p.m. That is the end of your workday. Shut 'er down.

Then you put your work devices in a room with the door closed and you leave them there. I was struggling with this until I figured out the warning bell. I print out my schedule for the next day, making sure I know what is coming and that I am prepared for it. Then I can close my office door and not give it another thought 'til the next morning.

You will feel twitchy at first, but you will start to enjoy it pretty quickly. It is life-changing.

FRESH FLOWERS

If you are allergic to flowers, this will not do at all.

If not, buy yourself some flowers next time you are at the

grocery store. You do not need a fancy vase (*"vahz"*). You can use a mason jar or a pitcher... *or* a fancy vase.

Put your flowers front and center so you can enjoy them. When I get flowers, I move them with me from room to room. I like to get the maximum amount of enjoyment from my flowers!

ESSENTIAL OIL DIFFUSER

Like scented candles, but with essential oils and a diffuser. Get it?

This one is fun because you can create your own recipe. There are all sorts of combinations to enjoy, or you can stick with just one simple scent. Whatever you want!

Maybe you have a full collection of essential oils or maybe you do not have any. I built mine up over time and am still adding. You can definitely start small!

———

✍ Do you already have some of these in place? If not, pick one or two. Notice how it makes a difference.

———

SELF-CARE MINIMALISM

I've got a mini chapter here to talk about self-care minimalism. See what I did there?

Most of us, myself included, can establish a solid self-care habit…

… as long as we are living our regular everyday life.

If something disrupts that pattern at all, it is possible (and likely, in my experience) that we waver and even disregard our self-care.

It could be vacation. It could be a family emergency. Maybe an illness. Sometimes it is a major change like divorce or a new job. It could be that we overslept.

It does not have to be a negative situation. You could be in a new relationship that has you over the moon with joy!

As you discover what your basic self-care needs are, meeting them will become routine. You will anticipate them, and your mind will desire the care.

You will need the routine. Those are the things you keep doing no matter what.

My tiniest self-care routine is my full skincare routine and a ten-to-fifteen-minute guided meditation. The whole thing takes me twenty minutes, start to finish. It is the least I can do to still feel cared for by myself. If I can, I add a stretching session to the end of the day.

I use this minimalist routine when I sleep too late to do my whole routine. I use it when I am feeling low. I use it when I am on vacation, whatever that is. If I do not get the meditation in first thing in the morning, I do it sometime during the day.

Play with your routine. Skip part of it for a few days and take note of how you feel. If you don't notice a difference, you may not need that part. Add something else. If you do miss the part you skipped, that means it's probably something you should include in your minimalist approach to self-care on days when you just don't have time for everything.

Figure out what your self-care minimalism is and do it. No matter what.

If you have a day when you can't get your routine in and you haven't planned your self-care mini-routine, pay attention to how you feel throughout your day. You'll most likely be a little bit off.

How do you think I came up with this idea?

———

✍ If you had to guess, what would your minimalist approach to routine be? Write that down. As you get to know your routines better, you can adjust it.

———

19

LET'S WRAP THIS UP

*I*n a bit, I am going to give you three things to do to get started on your self-care journey. You can pick the order you do them in, but do them all.

You have probably heard different things about how long it takes to create a habit. The most common one I had heard before I was in this line of work was twenty-one days. This is true for some things, but not true for others. The length of time it takes to create a habit depends on what level of change you are attempting.

It is a lot easier to build the habit of drinking a glass of water first thing in the morning than it is to create a habit of running for thirty minutes a day. Makes sense, right?

Creating a habit is wiring your brain. How long did it take you to wire your brain not to perform self-care? Your whole life.

The beauty of making a change is that, with intention, it will not take years. It does take consistency and effort on your part though. Self-care is a practice. You must keep making it a priority and sticking with it. You will start to notice the benefits before you are finished with the thirty-day challenge that comes next.

A funny thing humans do is, when they start to feel better, they stop doing what it was that made them feel better. We can be so silly!

When you start to feel better because you are taking care of yourself, keep doing it. Do more. Build some cushion for the tougher days.

As promised – your first assignment:

1. Complete the thirty-day challenge from the next section
2. Create your bedtime/ morning routines
3. Come up with your self-care minimalism

Complete these three steps over the next month and you will have the very baby beginnings of a self-care habit. The key to your success will be that you do not give up. You adjust.

You deserve it.

Remember: self-care is whatever you need it to be.

———

✍ Take some time and reconnect to why self-care is important to you. Go back to your notes from Chapter 7. How can you make the "why" even more empowering?

———

MY CHALLENGE TO YOU

Have fun with this!

Grab a notebook to keep track of your progress on this

challenge, or download a printable version here: https://yourapocalypse.com.

For each day, scheduling your self-care is part of the process, so pop it into your schedule in the morning. If you miss a day or five, just go back to the day before the one you missed and start again. If you feel like you need it, you can start at the beginning – any time you want!

What is the worst thing that could happen? You will enjoy more self-care!

When you get through all thirty days in a row, keep going and going and going! Add more.

You will have more energy, excitement, and enthusiasm and you will be able to do things you only wished you could do before you started treating yourself well. Tell all the women you know that they deserve to feel good and show them how to do it!

Day 1

_____ Morning intention:

Find three things today that make me smile.

_____ Five minutes of self-care:

What will I do?
What time will I do it?

_____Evening reflection:

What three things made me smile?
How do I feel about my five minutes of self-care?
What will I do differently tomorrow?
What will I do the same?

Day 2

_____ Morning intention:

Find three things today that I love about my home.

_____ Five minutes of self-care:

What will I do?
What time will I do it?

_____ Evening reflection:

What three things do I love about my home?
How do I feel about my five minutes of self-care?
What will I do differently tomorrow?
What will I do the same?

Day 3

_____ Morning intention:

Find three things today that I love about my work.

_____ Five minutes of self-care:

What will I do?
What time will I do it?

_____ Evening reflection:

What three things do I love about my work?
How do I feel about my five minutes of self-care?
What will I do differently tomorrow?

What will I do the same?

Day 4

_____ Morning intention:

Find a new way to enjoy a meal.

_____ Five minutes of self-care:

What will I do?
What time will I do it?

_____ Evening reflection:

How did I enjoy a meal differently today?
How do I feel about my five minutes of self-care?
What will I do differently tomorrow?
What will I do the same?

Day 5

_____ Morning intention:

Find my favorite thing about today.

_____ Five minutes of self-care – two times:

What will I do?
What time(s) will I do it?

_____ Evening reflection:

What is my favorite thing about today?

How do I feel about my ten minutes of self-care?
What will I do differently tomorrow?
What will I do the same?

Day 6

_____ Morning intention:

Come up with three reasons I deserve self-care.

_____ Five minutes of self-care – two times:

What will I do?
What time(s) will I do it?

_____ Evening reflection:

What are my three reasons for deserving self-care?
How do I feel about my ten minutes of self-care?
What will I do differently tomorrow?
What will I do the same?

Day 7

_____ Morning intention:

Let two people know I am grateful for them and tell them why.

_____ Five minutes of self-care – two times:

What will I do?
What time(s) will I do it?

_____ Evening reflection:

Who am I grateful for and why?
How do I feel about my ten minutes of self-care?
What will I do differently tomorrow?
What will I do the same?

Day 8

_____ Morning intention:

Notice three things I do well.

_____ Five minutes of self-care – two times:

What will I do?
What time(s) will I do it?

_____ Evening reflection:

What three things do I do well?
How do I feel about my ten minutes of self-care?
What will I do differently tomorrow?
What will I do the same?

Day 9

_____ Morning intention:

No complaining today.

_____ Five minutes of self-care – three times:

What will I do?

What time(s) will I do it?

_____ Evening reflection:

Did I complain today?
How do I feel about my fifteen minutes of self-care?
What will I do differently tomorrow?
What will I do the same?

Day 10

_____ Morning intention:

Notice three things I think are beautiful.

_____ Five minutes of self-care – three times:

What will I do?
What time(s) will I do it?

_____ Fifteen minutes of self-care:

What will I do?
What time will I do it?

_____ Evening reflection:

Did I complain today?
How do I feel about my thirty minutes of self-care?
What will I do differently tomorrow?
What will I do the same?

Day 11

_____ Morning intention:

Find three things to laugh about.

_____ Five minutes of self-care – three times:

What will I do?
What time(s) will I do it?

_____ Fifteen minutes of self-care:

What will I do?
What time will I do it?

_____ Evening reflection:

How was laughing?
How do I feel about my thirty minutes of self-care?
What will I do differently tomorrow?
What will I do the same?

Day 12

_____ Morning intention:

Get up and move around throughout the day.

_____ Five minutes of self-care – three times:

What will I do?
What time(s) will I do it?

_____ Fifteen minutes of self-care:

What will I do?
What time will I do it?

_____ Evening reflection:

How did I move my body?
How do I feel about my thirty minutes of self-care?
What will I do differently tomorrow?
What will I do the same?

Day 13

_____ Morning intention:

Think about what I would do if I could not fail.

_____ Five minutes of self-care – three times:

What will I do?
What time(s) will I do it?

_____ Fifteen minutes of self-care:

What will I do?
What time will I do it?

_____ Evening reflection:

What would I do if I could not fail?
How do I feel about my thirty minutes of self-care?
What will I do differently tomorrow?
What will I do the same?

Day 14

_____ Morning intention:

Find five things today that make me smile.

_____ Five minutes of self-care – three times:

What will I do?
What time(s) will I do it?

_____ Fifteen minutes of self-care:

What will I do?
What time will I do it?

_____ Evening reflection:

What made me smile?
How do I feel about my thirty minutes of self-care?
What will I do differently tomorrow?
What will I do the same?

Day 15

_____ Morning intention:

Find a way to connect with someone today.

_____ Five minutes of self-care – three times:

What will I do?
What time(s) will I do it?

_____ Fifteen minutes of self-care – two times:

What will I do?
What time(s) will I do it?

_____ Evening reflection:

Who did I connect with?
How do I feel about my forty-five minutes of self-care?
What will I do differently tomorrow?
What will I do the same?

Day 16

_____ Morning intention:

Think of three memories that make me happy.

_____ Five minutes of self-care – three times:

What will I do?
What time(s) will I do it?

_____ Fifteen minutes of self-care – two times:

What will I do?
What time(s) will I do it?

_____ Evening reflection:

What are my memories and why do they make me happy?
How do I feel about my forty-five minutes of self-care?
What will I do differently tomorrow?
What will I do the same?

Day 17

_____ Morning intention:

I will play some music that makes me feel good today.

_____ Five minutes of self-care – three times:

What will I do?
What time(s) will I do it?

_____ Fifteen minutes of self-care – two times:

What will I do?
What time(s) will I do it?

_____ Evening reflection:

What is the best song I heard today and why?
How do I feel about my forty-five minutes of self-care?
What will I do differently tomorrow?
What will I do the same?

Day 18

_____ Morning intention:

I will speak to myself with love today.

_____ Five minutes of self-care – three times:

What will I do?
What time(s) will I do it?

_____ Fifteen minutes of self-care – two times:

What will I do?
What time(s) will I do it?

_____ Evening reflection:

How did it feel to be kind to myself?
How do I feel about my forty-five minutes of self-care?
What will I do differently tomorrow?
What will I do the same?

Day 19

_____ Morning intention:

I will be gentle with myself today.

_____ Five minutes of self-care – three times:

What will I do?
What time(s) will I do it?

_____ Fifteen minutes of self-care – two times:

What will I do?
What time(s) will I do it?

_____ Evening reflection:

How and when did I need to be gentle with myself?
How do I feel about my forty-five minutes of self-care?
What will I do differently tomorrow?
What will I do the same?

Day 20

_____ Morning intention:

I will be my biggest supporter today.

_____ Five minutes of self-care – three times:

What will I do?
What time(s) will I do it?

_____ Fifteen minutes of self-care – two times:

What will I do?
What time(s) will I do it?

_____ Evening reflection:

When did I need my support and how did I support myself?
How do I feel about my forty-five minutes of self-care?
What will I do differently tomorrow?
What will I do the same?

Day 21

_____ Morning intention:

I will be curious about what I need.

_____ Five minutes of self-care – three times:

What will I do?
What time(s) will I do it?

_____ Fifteen minutes of self-care – three times:

What will I do?
What time(s) will I do it?

_____ Evening reflection:

What did I notice that I needed and how did I provide that for myself?
How do I feel about my hour (*WOOOHOOOO*!!) of self-care?
What will I do differently tomorrow?
What will I do the same?

Day 22

_____ Morning intention:

I will enjoy my food today.

_____ Five minutes of self-care – three times:

What will I do?
What time(s) will I do it?

_____ Fifteen minutes of self-care – three times:

What will I do?
What time(s) will I do it?

_____ Evening reflection:

What was the best thing I ate today?
How do I feel about my hour of self-care?

What will I do differently tomorrow?
What will I do the same?

Day 23

_____ Morning intention:

I will reach out to a friend today.

_____ Five minutes of self-care – three times:

What will I do?
What time(s) will I do it?

_____ Fifteen minutes of self-care – three times:

What will I do?
What time(s) will I do it?

_____ Evening reflection:

Who did I reach out to and how did it go?
How do I feel about my hour of self-care?
What will I do differently tomorrow?
What will I do the same?

Day 24

_____ Morning intention:

Today, I will pay attention to my energy and honor myself, wherever it is.

_____ Five minutes of self-care – three times:

What will I do?
What time(s) will I do it?

_____ Fifteen minutes of self-care – three times:

What will I do?
What time(s) will I do it?

_____ Evening reflection:

What did I notice about my energy and how did I honor myself?
How do I feel about my hour of self-care?
What will I do differently tomorrow?
What will I do the same?

Day 25

_____ Morning intention:

I will celebrate my progress today.

_____ Five minutes of self-care – three times:

What will I do?
What time(s) will I do it?

_____ Fifteen minutes of self-care – three times:

What will I do?
What time(s) will I do it?

_____ Evening reflection:

What and how did I celebrate?
How do I feel about my hour of self-care?
What will I do differently tomorrow?
What will I do the same?

Day 26

_____ Morning intention:

I will make someone laugh today.

_____ Five minutes of self-care – three times:

What will I do?
What time(s) will I do it?

_____ Fifteen minutes of self-care – three times:

What will I do?
What time(s) will I do it?

_____ Evening reflection:

Who did I make laugh and how did it feel?
How do I feel about my hour of self-care?
What will I do differently tomorrow?
What will I do the same?

Day 27

_____ Morning intention:

I will enjoy myself today.

_____ Five minutes of self-care – six times:

What will I do?
What time(s) will I do it?

_____ Fifteen minutes of self-care – three times:

What will I do?
What time(s) will I do it?

_____ Evening reflection:

What did I enjoy about myself today?
How do I feel about my hour and fifteen minutes of self-care?
What will I do differently tomorrow?
What will I do the same?

Day 28

_____ Morning intention:

I will find five things I love about my body.

_____ Five minutes of self-care – six times:

What will I do?
What time(s) will I do it?

_____ Fifteen minutes of self-care – three times:

What will I do?
What time(s) will I do it?

_____ Evening reflection:

What is awesome about my body?
How do I feel about my hour and fifteen minutes of self-care?
What will I do differently tomorrow?
What will I do the same?

Day 29

_____ Morning intention:

I will find ten things that make me smile.

_____ Five minutes of self-care – six times:

What will I do?
What time(s) will I do it?

_____ Fifteen minutes of self-care – three times:

What will I do?
What time(s) will I do it?

_____ Evening reflection:

What made me smile today?
How do I feel about my hour and fifteen minutes of self-care?
What will I do differently tomorrow?
What will I do the same?

Day 30

_____ Morning intention:

I will treat myself like the queen I am!

_____ Five minutes of self-care – six times:

What will I do?
What time(s) will I do it?

_____ Fifteen minutes of self-care – three times:

What will I do?
What time(s) will I do it?

_____ Evening reflection:

What was my royal treatment for the day?
How do I feel about my hour and fifteen minutes of self-care?
What will I do differently tomorrow?
What will I do the same?

20

AND THAT, MY FRIEND, IS ALL SHE WROTE

*Y*ou've made it here – welcome to the end of the book. Thank you for giving yourself the time and attention you truly deserve.

Remember, you *do* deserve it. If that's still a bit wobbly, remember that those around you deserve the best version of you, and that can only happen if you take care of yourself first.

Do the thirty-day challenge – more than once if you need it. Keep building your habit. Don't stop at thirty minutes – go for an hour... and three hours... and a day... on and on!

Keep this book handy, and let it remind you how amazing you are. Take ideas from it. Reread the parts you love, and even the parts you don't, because repetition is the mother of all skill. And self-care... it's a skill indeed. Master it.

On days when you feel overwhelmed or get bad news... turbo-boost the self-care. On days when you feel great... don't skimp on your self-care.

As you grow your self-care habit, notice how life around you changes.

You are the creator of your life. Make sure you get to enjoy it.

You deserve it.

SOME THANKS

There is really no way I will be able express my gratitude fully, but I am going to say thank you anyway. So many people have impacted my life and helped me get here, to a place where I can impact others. My list is mostly chronological and first names only – I hope you know who you are already.

With a full heart of gratitude, I thank: Mike, Teri, Kelly, Emily, Austin, Bob, Dotty, Margaret, Carl, Jan, Carl, Kay, Ron, Bob, Penny, Mark, Mike, Rick, Greg, Heather, Betty, Howard, Another Betty, Jeannette, Becky, Kat, Dick, Drew, Randy, Andy, Lisa, Arin, Jeff, Rex, Austin, Vicki, Shellie, Rusty, Kaspar, Eve, Julia, Samantha, Rebecca, Matt, Jeff, Rob, Steve, Austin, Brian, Gina, Terry, Kristin, Eric, Gary, Mike, Carly, Madelyn, Izzy, Sara, Ann, Jeff, Colin, Luann, Jean, Kathy, Pam, Dawn, Guy, Sandra, Amy, Jon, Courtney, Gary, Chris, JLo, Tonia, Jerry, Another Dawn, Natasha, Sabrina, Maria, Dora, Steve, Kelsie, Stephani, Nick, Sandra, Bob, Sallie, Michelle, Meredith, Jodi, Rob, Elizabeth, Piper, Tammie, Karla, Laura, Tony, Elaine, Brenda, Tad, Steve, Chris, Elizabeth, Linda, Julie, Stacy, Trevor, Daniel, Tom, Rosa, Bonnie, Amy, Karolynn, Mandi, Lauren, Carol, Maria (M), Kippie, Kelly, Hannah, Linda, and Carine.

ABOUT THE AUTHOR

Having gone through many of her own personal apocalypses, Jennifer has made it her life's work to help other women connect to their joy so they can design the lives they deserve. She spends most of her time at home these days (since it's a pandemic and she's an introvert). Her days are divided between her amazing clients, being a mom to two badass daughters, emptying litter boxes, and whatever the hell she needs for self-care. Her dream is to launch her daughters into the world full of confidence and joy. After that, she imagines, she will move into a tiny home on wheels so she can live wherever she wants. Once upon a time, her dream was to write a book, so she's really looking forward to life on the road.

Jennifer wants you to dream big *and* take care of yourself. You deserve it.

PSST... ONE MORE THING!

Parting is such sweet sorrow. I'm not ready to say goodbye! I love a long-term relationship and hope you do too. I'll be around doing my best to come up with new ways to shine more light into the world. Check me out on the interwebs at https://yourapocalypse.com

Let me know how your life changes once you've made yourself a priority – I love reader stories! Want to take your life to the next level? Sign up for a discovery session with me – I'd love that, too!

Made in the USA
Columbia, SC
04 March 2021

33900065R00112